C000076004

BILL'S BEAT

A Biography

BILL'S BEAT

A Biography

BROWN
DOG
BOOKS

First published 2018

Copyright © Bernard Mullin 2018

The right of Bernard Mullin to be identified as the author of this work has been asserted in accordance with the Copyright, Designs & Patents Act 1988.

All rights reserved. No part of this book may be reproduced, stored in a retrieval system, or transmitted in any form or by any means, electronic, electrostatic, magnetic tape, mechanical, photocopying, recording or otherwise, without the written permission of the copyright holder.

Published under licence by Brown Dog Books and
The Self-Publishing Partnership, 7 Green Park Station, Bath BA1 1JB

www.selfpublishingpartnership.co.uk

ISBN printed book: 978-1-78545-308-3

ISBN e-book: 978-1-78545-309-0

Cover design by Mark Alexander

Internal design by Jenny Watson Design

Printed and bound by CPI Group (UK) Ltd, Croydon, CR0 4YY

This book is dedicated to my late mother, Mrs Mabel Mullin (nee Lewin) who inspired me to write about PC 'Bill' Gutteridge.

ACKNOWLEDGMENTS

I offer my special thanks to Mr Brian Alexander, Stephen and Christopher Gutteridge and their families for giving me permission to write a biographical work on their grandfather, PC George William Gutteridge including that of his wife Rose who, following her husband's murder endured little known and very great hardship for the selfless sake of her children. I would also like to thank them for the friendship and hospitality they have shown me throughout my extensive research into the lives of their grandparents. I feel humbled that they have trusted and supported me wholly in my quest to pay tribute to their grandparents through my work, but predominantly to maintain the memory of the late PC George William 'Bill' Gutteridge of the Essex County Constabulary 1889–1927.

DISCLAIMER

All incidents and occurrences are factual accounts sourced through much research from original archived documentation held at the Essex Police Museum in Chelmsford and other reputable sources of research which has been acknowledged and to whom I offer my sincere gratitude for all their assistance in this work.

My intention has always been to pay tribute to PC George Gutteridge and his wife Rose, the communities in which they lived and those who knew them in a wide spectrum of situations as accurately as possible and I apologise for any errata. Over nearly 90 years, many versions have entered the pages of a number of publications portraying the murder and some inaccurate aspects of the life PC George Gutteridge including, of course his untimely and brutal death. So, it has remained my aim to shine the spotlight on the lives of George and Rose Gutteridge and illustrate, as accurately as possible 'snapshots' of their lives before they met, their relatively short marriage, and their time together in Stapleford Abbotts. The tenacity, bravery, hardship and dedication they experienced in their tragically brief lives together is beyond question.

CONTENTS

FOREWORD

By Brian Alexander

When Bernard told me he wanted to write a book about my grandfather, the late PC George William Gutteridge known as 'Bill', I thought that there was no more to be said as it had been written and told over and over again and has been on the radio and even filmed. What more can be added to a horrendous incident that happened to a police officer doing his job, upholding the law and protecting the community, whose life came to a tragic end in the early hours of September the 27th 1927, the morning that changed the lives forever of those that were involved with the incident and those related to Bill. One change was for a now-homeless mother with her two children, Muriel and Alfred, (known as Jack). Another change, as the family had to move following this incident, affected Muriel as she had lost her childhood sweetheart, John Alexander, who lived next door to her at No.3 Towneley Cottages, Stapleford Abbotts.

Fortunately for Muriel, this would eventually change for the better as many years later, John found a job working at The Ford Motor Company in Dagenham and he soon discovered that his childhood sweetheart also lived there and just by chance they met up again. They eventually married in 1938 and it was in the evening of 26th April 1944 during an air raid that I decided to enter the world as the first grandchild of George Gutteridge.

George has three other grandchildren one of which is his only granddaughter, Muriel, my sister. George's son Jack has two sons,

Stephen and Christopher. Grandad's family has since extended to great grandchildren and even great great-grandchildren.

Bernard explained to me what the book was to be about; the life of the Gutteridge's before and after that awful incident. He has gone to great lengths with his research, to the extent of becoming a member of numerous societies and other organisations in order to write this book. Bernard was brought up in Collier Row, Essex, near Romford. He spent a lot of his childhood, like me, in Stapleford Abbotts. One of his relations owned the little sweetshop near Towneley Cottages at the bottom of Tysea Hill on the corner of Oak Hill Road. I find Bernard to be a fine gentleman. He has lots of passion and has been very dedicated to this project and has asked me many questions. The answers that I have given have been passed down to me by my mother, who rarely spoke about her family's past. Thanks to Bernard, I have now found out a lot more about how life had been for her, her mother and younger brother. I am unable to comprehend how painful it must have been for her to talk about it as she had lost her daddy when she was twelve years old whilst her little brother had only just had his fourth birthday a week earlier.

A very big thank you to you Bernie for your compassion, patience and utmost dedication. You have managed to put together a massive jigsaw of history of which many of the pieces were missing. You have become a true friend.

Granddad may you rest in peace.

Brian Alexander

The author with Mr Brian Alexander at the 'Top Oak' in 2015

INTRODUCTION

Sometimes, ideas lie dormant in the mind for a short time or for many years and in my case it is the latter. A seed unwittingly sown in my subconscious as a child by my mother, Mabel Mullin (nee Lewin) who was 7 years old when PC 'Bill' Gutteridge met his fate on the Romford to Ongar road near to the home of my grandparents, John and Ellen Lewin where she lived with her brothers and sisters. Many years later my mother would speak with sorrow in her voice telling us children about 'poor PC Gutteridge' and how, in her detailed description he was found dead at the side of the road by the postman. Although Alec Ward was, of course, not the postman (as this was Harry Alexander at 3 Towneley Cottages). Alec delivered mail bags to a number of Post Offices in the area in addition to his many other activities at his Warley garage premises so understandably as a child, my mother may have innocently been told that Alec *was* the postman whose horrific discovery brought him an unenviable fame in finding the dead body of his long time friend Bill Gutteridge. This gruesome discovery was made so much worse for Alec in discovering later to his growing horror that his friend Bill Gutteridge's eyes had been shot out by the assailant in the superstitious and scientifically unproven misbelief that the eyes retain the last image seen before death (referred to as an optogram) and therefore may have provided a form of 'photographic' evidence which may have convicted his killer or killers.

PC George Gutteridge was another policeman working for the good of his community in the lean years between the wars and was only known at that time to the people of Wimbotsham and Downham Market in west Norfolk, the Southend-on-Sea area of coastal Essex,

Grays and as a village policeman in Stapleford Abbotts, a now very different village to what it was, but still to this day retaining an infrastructure of vibrant community life.

But as is very well documented, the peace of this small village was to be shattered on the morning of the 27th September 1927 when a wave of national and to some extent, international public outrage focussed the spotlight on Stapleford Abbotts in the wake of the needless and brutal murder of PC Bill Gutteridge. With the passage of time and the passing of many of the older residents of the village, vivid memories of the 1920s have faded, but in true Essex village tradition many have retained personal and handed-down valuable recollections of those far distant times and how very different local society was then. Education, personal values and respect for others was central to the dedicated work of PC Bill Gutteridge, a man with a firm persona tenaciously upholding the law in the village of Stapleford Abbotts and whose brutal demise left a huge void in a village numb with shock and disbelief.

He was not perfect, known within his community for a bit of poaching when off duty in addition to his love of a frequent pint of beer at the Rabbits and the Top Oak but the impression he left on this close rural community endures, with his perceived shortcomings falling away to reveal the true spirit of this special man. Still revered to this day, his untimely death has firmly placed Stapleford Abbotts in the annals of the history of crime, the advent of the '999' emergency call system and for the first time in this country, ballistics evidence being used to great effect by gun and ballistics expert Mr. Robert Churchill, who proved beyond any doubt that the empty cartridge case found in Dr. Lovell's car came from the gun found in the possession of Frederick Guy Browne and his accomplice, William Henry Kennedy. This was conclusive and they paid the ultimate price for their crime with their lives on the 31st. May 1928 being hanged at the same moment at Pentonville and Wandsworth prisons respectively.

Over 90 years of speculation and theories of 'who was actually guilty and at the of the murder have been aired, and there still exists some 'question marks' as to the joint culpability of Browne and Kennedy in this very deliberate act of murder of a very respected village policeman.

This book is not intended to revisit or examine the murder or theorise on aspects of the crime itself as has been done many, many, times in various publications over the years including many 'attachments' having been added to various accounts. However, the main aim is to produce a biographical work on the life of Bill Gutteridge from his Norfolk roots to the premature end of his life. It is also my intention to illustrate the commitment to duty and the zeal he demonstrated toward his police duties in the village he took to his heart, Stapleford Abbotts and I would strongly suggest, fuelled through an innate love for his wife Rose, Muriel and Alfred, their children, who endured much hardship in the aftermath of George's murder.

This book also represents a dual tribute not only to a dedicated and loyal family man who, in the prime of his life at 38 years old was killed for the principles of law and order he held in high regard, but for the personal and social values for which he stood.

Bill had left Rose, a true legacy of love to this, his loyal and dedicated wife who, unknown to many was cast adrift to fend for herself and her children in her early widow-hood with minimal help from the authorities; the void of the loss of Bill being partially filled with the love and support of close family and friends most notably Agnes and Frank Cross, Minnie and Frank Meadows with Harry and Ethel Alexander and their children. The weight Rose took upon her shoulders after the terrible loss of Bill and the strength she displayed in keeping her dignity intact and family together in very austere times would have broken lesser beings at the first post. Rose singularly sacrificed all for her children, 'going without food so they could eat, never remarrying or having any men friends', to quote the late Muriel Alexander in talking about her mother in later years.

Like George, who did not shy from his assailants, Rose could have taken the easy way out when the police authorities strongly 'encouraged' her to put her children, especially little Alfred (Jack) - stating that boys were 'harder to bring up' - into the Police School, (an orphanage run by the police authorities) which would take some pressure off her situation. But Rose, sensing that this would very likely permanently remove her children from her care, put the authorities firmly in their place by ardently refusing their offer and assertively telling them she would look after her children herself. George was the only one she loved and with him gone she 'held the fort' admirably with love and determination until she was quietly reunited with George in their joint resting place in grave B131 at Lorne Road Cemetery in 1956.

CHAPTER 1

EARLY DAYS

The Beautifully Carved and Ornate Sign On The Village Green at Wimbotsham.

Photo by author

Wimbotsham, is a short distance south of Downham Market in Norfolk and just off the busy A10 between King's Lynn and Cambridge. It is a small, popular and thriving village nestling on the edge of the Fens overlooked proudly by the church of St. Mary the Virgin (pictured) standing on the high ground as you enter the village by the meandering Church Road which leads down to the hub of the village where the green is host to the Chequers Pub and the village hall all within yards of each other.

The beautiful Church of St. Mary the Virgin, Wimbotsham.

Picture by author

Wimbotsham Village Green in around 1900. The village sign visible to the centre left of the picture. By kind courtesy of Mr Christopher Shaw, Historian, the TW Mollard Collection and the Downham Market and District Heritage Society.

The Chequers Public House, Wimbotsham in later years
but the fabric is largely unchanged.

By kind courtesy of Mr Christopher Shaw, Historian, the TW Mollard Collection
and the Downham Market and District Heritage Society

Wimbotsham Village School pictured in 1900. George is not in this picture . as he attended
the Board School at nearby Denver where he was staying with his grandparents.

By kind courtesy of Mr Christopher Shaw, Historian, the TW Mollard Collection
and the Downham Market and District Heritage Society

But over the years, Wimbotsham has grown in stature becoming rather an annual 'Mecca' for all on two wheels and many visitors with four! On August bank holiday Mondays the village has become famous within the national motorcycling calendar for hosting The Fenman Classic Bike Show; an annual classic motorcycle event. This glittering and, in some cases, not so glittering display of every kind of two-wheeled transport from the humble Mobylette moped from the sixties to the chrome-laden Harley Davidsons, is certainly very evocative especially for those in later life whose work and social transport had been a motorbike; the sound, the smell, often the discomfort and of course, the oil leaks! All this still holds a plethora of memories and just the sight of an old BSA or Triumph is very evocative to many of us in later years.

A 1915 triumph motorcycle and wickerwork sidecar reminiscent of the outfit John Alexander described that George used to take his and the Alexander children out for rides on days he was off-duty around the local country lanes.

Courtesy of: www.Magnell.org New Zealand and Australia

However, on a summer's day on the 29th July 1889, a different sound was heard to that of the roar of motorcycle engines as, in a rented cottage near the village green in this small village, the shrill cry of a baby boy could be heard; born out of wedlock to a 19-year-old mother and destined for a posthumous, tragic and lasting fame for bravery.

Born George William, to Mary Gutteridge a general domestic servant, born in 1870 in the nearby village of Denver, to John and Maria Gutteridge, George was to take his mother's maiden surname in the absence of a father whose identity to date has not been established.

Photo by author

The name Gutteridge is familiar in the Downham Market area with five graves in the church of St. Mary the Virgin Wimbotsham, clearly displaying the surname Gutteridge, one of which dates from the 1920s, interestingly, also marking the final resting place of another George William Gutteridge (no relation evident) who died in 1922 aged 44 and two days later, his father Thomas died aged 77. Why they died only a few days apart is unclear and it has been speculated that injuries sustained in an industrial accident may have been the result but as Dr Chipperfield suggests in her thesis on the murder of PC Gutteridge, the slow recession of the 'Spanish Flu' of 1918 or a localised outbreak of cholera may have claimed two more victims. By april 1891 Mary had moved with little George into a two-room accommodation close to the brickyards and gasworks in the industrial area of the increasingly prosperous town of Downham Market, now working as needleworker in a shirt factory as is recorded in the census of that year.

As George was now only approximately one year old it is most likely that as an infant he was cared for by his grandparents John and Maria Gutteridge who were now living in Wimbotsham whilst Mary was at work. Around ten years later Mary had moved again to Priory Cottages in Downham and had married a Mr. Ambrose of whom little is known but the name Ambrose is familiar in Denver.

Their marriage was very brief with Mr Ambrose leaving Mary to fend for herself but thankfully she was able to enlist the help of her younger sister Alice to help with the day to day running of the house while she worked.

Mary remarried for a short time but it did not last due to her husband's drinking habits and by 1928 and at 59 years old, following a period of separation during which she had to survive on a regular allowance from him of 7 shillings and sixpence and having to supplement her income by taking on small domestic jobs such as sewing and cleaning, Mary found herself widowed.

Young George had an elementary education at the Board School in Denver as required by law. [The Education Act of 1870, introduced by Liberal MP William Forster with attendance not being made compulsory for children up to the age of 13 until 1880 (with some exceptions), provided an opportunity for working people to advance themselves with some basic elementary education with the option of extra tuition from teachers if the parents could afford it or alternatively from adult education organisations and worker's societies.] George must have been reasonably well taught as were his young uncles with whom he went to school; 12-year-old Walter and 13-year-old Arthur

Gutteridge in the disciplined, but limited education he received although his official police record of service is devoid of any state educational record.

He must however, have shown some potential as original archived material written by George as a policeman demonstrates a clear, reasonable writing style and grasp of spelling and grammar albeit this was limited, and was to hold him back academically and financially when he sat his sergeants' exam in later years. School did not attract George, rather he had to, as a boy and especially without a father figure, take on the mantle of 'man of the house' to some extent and support his mother in any way he could financially in the lean years of 1880s and 1900s rural Norfolk working class society.

It was here in the Downham Market area of west Norfolk that George met Rose Savill, a girl three years older than himself and who had stolen his heart when they were children together in the closely adjacent villages of Ryston to the south of Downham where Alfred and Sarah Savill, with their children, had been reposted to the remote cottage and railway crossing in this very small village (the terms of his employment as a railway gatekeeper required Alfred to work wherever he was needed), and Denver, where John and Maria Gutteridge now lived with little George, still a small child spending much time here with his grandparents whilst his mother Mary was working in Downham Market a short distance away. At only eight years old George's working life began to help support his single mother financially whilst still attending school. Thankfully, he was resourceful, fit and strong and even as a child not frightened to 'roll up his sleeves' and earn some money which he began in1897 as a handyman for the local baptist minister, the Rev. Samuel Howard, very much a philanthropist, champion of education for the poor and a kindly family man of advancing years who lived at the Manse in Bexwell Road, Downham Market.

A poor quality, but rare picture of the wife (second from left) and family of the Rev. Samuel Howard outside their home in Bexwell Road, Downham market.

Courtesy Downham Market and District Heritage Society

The Howard home as it is today in Bexwell Road.

Courtesy of the Downham Market and District Heritage Society

Baptist Church Sunday School ready with buckets and spades for their treat to Hunstanton in 1923. The coach was supplied by Mr B. Mace of Shouldham

It is believed that the The Rev. Samuel Howard is included in thispicture of a Sunday School outing in 1923.

Courtesy of the Downham Market and District Heritage society

The Rev. Howard could obviously see that George was genuine in his desire to help his struggling mother Mary cope financially but also with the social stigma of being an unmarried mother, even at such a young age, and this must have impressed him enough to give George some occasional paid work.

Now, realising that if he worked hard, the rewards of his labours would come to fruition, he continued in this way. As he was growing up and having left school at around 14 years old, he followed the example of his grandfather and uncles by entering the building trade and was employed in 1899 as a labourer by HB Mash Builders to expand his talents further (Mr Mash being an officer and Superintendent Inspector with the Downham Market Urban District Council). Bitten by the 'work bug' and the prospect of further income he added to this, working with J.W. Collins another local builder, in the Downham Market area. George spread his wings even further by adding the firm of John Vince Long, Stone and Marble Mason of nearby Church lane in Downham Market to his growing circuit of local employers and which would be his last civilian employment before joining the police.

John (Johnny) Vince Long's yard in Church Lane Downham Market.

Courtesy, The TW Mollard Collection, Downham Market and district Heritage Society

George developed his skills further by working as a bricklayer and labourer for Mr. Long, a relatively short distance from his own home, now at No.4 Priory Cottages in Priory Road, Downham Market where he still lodged for part of the time with his mother and who had now married for the second time, becoming Mrs Mary Edwards. It is evident from local records of the time that George must have been well respected as a reliable and capable worker because several of his employers held high office in the local community and probably had the choice of many young men to employ who were looking for work in those lean years, understandably calling only on those who were sober of nature and to be relied upon. It appears that George was a popular choice possibly reinforced by the knowledge that George's family had an already established and reliable reputation in the building trade locally.

George's employers were astute in recognising the potential in a young man who, it could be said, at 8 years old, forwent a proportion of childhood play and probably regular education in favour of paid work to support his single mother and himself.

Downham Market, much like a host of other small towns and villages then and now, was close knit with news travelling fast by word of mouth through a very active 'grapevine' with local knowledge confirming that the young George Gutteridge was reliable, tenacious and hardworking in completing the tasks required of him. Official and informal photographs of George depict him as a no-nonsense character with a stern demeanour complemented by a strong physique developed through hard and often gruelling manual labour carried out in all that the Norfolk weather could throw at him. Some accounts depict him as 'a great bull of a man' standing 5ft. 10inches with a chest measurement of 37 inches. As will be seen later this physical and psychological strength would pay many dividends in his brief army career but as a policeman these qualities would prove to be particularly vital. George was a streetwise and resourceful young man; he had to be, like many others in his situation he knew this and worked hard until other opportunities to advance himself appeared on the horizon; acquiring some very useful and transferable skills such as stonecutting, bricklaying and carpentry within the wide-ranging building and maintenance work he performed for his employers.

The spectre of the workhouse was faced by those without employment in the days before the advent of the welfare state, with the poor having to rely on charity from the community or the church until this ceased by the passing of the Poor Law Amendment Act in1834 and the establishment of what was to be known and feared as the Union Workhouse system. (A union of local parishes who by law were grouped together and were required to build a workhouse for the destitute and needy.) These were approximately 20 miles apart depending upon the region and number of the population. The Union Workhouse in London road, Downham Market was a very attractive building, (as were many) and demolished in the 1960s to make way for housing for the elderly.

Courtesy of 'Peter Higginbotham / workhouses.org.uk'

But the reputation of these Dickensian institutions brought about by the Poor Law Amendment Act of 1834 must have been a very fearful, daunting and demoralising sight to those about to enter and who found themselves with little other choice. These poor individuals and families were often open to humiliation, exploitation and various forms of physical and mental abuse.

They lived, or more accurately, 'survived' on a very basic diet which they had to 'earn' by completing work targets for that day with families being segregated into men-only and women--only 'wards'; children being removed to separate dormitories upon entry but given education in very austere and strict workhouse schools. Adults could be forced to perform repetitive, hard and mind-numbing work such as 'picking oakem' (removing strands of flax from old ropes which would be mixed with tar and used in boatyards to seal leaking joints in wooden ships and clinker-built boats), to earn their keep in very unattractive and depressing surroundings; all on the basis that the authorities viewed unemployment to be a 'crime' with inmates being regarded as 'layabouts' and 'workshy'. In essence, being punished for the poverty stricken situation they found themselves in and most often not of their own making. However, it is fair to state that not all workhouses were identical, with some providing, although spartan and with little or no heating, a home of sorts to the poor and destitute where they at least could rely on meagre meals rather than starve and have the benefit of a roof over their heads, but the level of compassion given to the poor was often reliant on the personal values of the workhouse governor and the level of humanitarianism his regime would allow.

Very often, people and certainly girls needed to travel relatively large distances to gain employment as was the case with Rose 'Nettie' Savill, a Cambridgeshire girl now in service and destined to be the future wife of George. Rose was born in March 1887 into a continually growing family of nine very creatively named siblings, the daughter of Sarah and Alfred Savill, who by 1901 was still employed by the Great Eastern Railway Company as a railway gatekeeper as he had been at other locations as required by the terms of his employment.

The family had now relocated to the (then small) village of Fordham, a short distance from the growing fenland towns of Newmarket and Ely. Rose was only 17 when her mother died in 1904 aged 55 leaving Alfred to bring up the remaining (at home) family members on his own. This must have been a terrible blow for Rose and the Savill family but a further and much sadder loss struck with the sudden loss of Christina, the elder sister of Rose, who died suddenly in tragic circumstances aged 26 on the 4th December 1907. But for 21 year-old Rose, this tragedy could not compare with the nightmare which would befall her years hence on the morning of the 27th September 1927.

Christina, who had suffered poor health for some time and apparently had suffered fits in the past had disappeared that evening and with growing concern for her wellbeing, her father Alfred went out into the dark and rainy night to search for his daughter, meeting a neighbour Elizabeth Meadows who accompanied Alfred on his search. As they walked by the railway line Elizabeth spotted the hat bearing a red flower, that Christina was accustomed to wear and to their horror, lay the body of this young woman, his daughter, between the railway lines.

The circumstances surrounding her death remained a mystery and inconclusive. Speculation concerning her mental health would dominate her tragic demise and as Dr Chipperfield points out; 'Autopsies were not then performed in every case of sudden death, so Mrs Meadow's evidence that she, [Christina] was not 'in trouble' (a euphemism for being pregnant), was not corroborated by a post mortem result'. Without a mother to confide in or her sisters to talk to who were all away in service at the time, poor Christina's death is still shrouded in mystery. Alfred and his wife Sarah are now at rest, buried close to the grave of their daughter Christina in Fordham cemetery.

The grave of Christia Savill, Rose's sister.

Picture by author

The proud church of St. Peter and St. Mary Magdalene, Fordham Cambs.

Picture by author

The beautifully maintained pulpit at St. Mary Magdalene.

Picture by author

CHAPTER 2

GEORGE CHOOSES ESSEX FOR HIS POLICE CAREER

George worked hard in the years between 1897 until 1910 but in early April 1908 had to deal with the death of his 63-year-old Grandmother Maria Gutteridge who with her husband John, had often looked after him as a young child while their unmarried daughter Mary worked. Never idle and concurrent with his work,George had enlisted on the14 th September 1909 for a period of approximately five months as Lance Corporal 6602 Gutteridge in the 3rd Battallion Norfolk Regiment (Special Reserve) in Downham Market which would subsequently support his entry to the police force as applicants with military experience or as a reservist, in the case of George, would be given preference as they had already undergone military training not unlike the police training which he was soon to undergo.

In years to follow, this would also assist his entry to the Machine Gun Corps during his compulsory war service in World War One. George made his application to the Essex County Constabulary and what transpired answered a long since asked question as to why he had chosen Essex over Norfolk for his new police career? George wanted to be with the girl he first fell in love with during his schooldays and for him, his new career would be in Essex as he had found out through the grapevine that Rose was now working there in service for Stewart Forrest, the postmaster of Westcliff-on-Sea.

The Cap Badge of the Norfolk Regiment in the Great War. George is seen wearing his at Clipstone Camp in the group photo with other policemen.

Courtesy of the Norfolk Regiment

By the time they eventually met each other again Rose was in service at Crowstone Manor for a Mr Rumsey of Crowstone Road, Westcliff.

There was no other choice for George, whose heart had made the decision for him! But always aware of financial constraints of intermittent employment even in the booming building trade in his home town and aware that illness or worse, long term injury could leave him penniless long before the full introduction of the welfare state benefits system, he also needed job security. This was of course the stark reality (unless you paid into one of the 'friendly' societies in the event that you found yourself unemployed) many years before the beginning of the National Health Service in1948 tenaciously fought for by politician and humanitarian social reformer, Aneurin Bevan.

George must have considered this a logical, shrewd move in pursuing his objectives of eventually marrying Rose and providing her with some financial security in their lives together with a regular and comparatively well paid pensionable job.

Satisfactory references followed from his four different employers, consistent in their individual and unrelated responses in reflecting their satisfaction with his reliability, performance and sobriety but implying that he could be of a surly disposition and 'put out' (become angry) if crossed, and he was accepted into the police force.

On the 5th April 1910, 20-year-old George was appointed Constable and on the 6th April he was officially discharged as a reservist from the Norfolk Regiment. On the 8th of April 1910 PC 489 George William Gutteridge was officially sworn in with the Essex Constabulary and after spending one month of quite intensive training at Chelmsford Police headquarters during which George had to 'cram' the basics of police procedure, drill and discipline (an aspect of his training that would not be a shock to army reservist George), the fundamentals of the most common Acts which he would need to be familiar with and indeed the recording and form filling which would accompany his work, his police career began in earnest at the seaside town of Southend-on-Sea on the 2nd of May of the same year.

He enjoyed a starting wage of £1 2s 2d, approximately £100 in todays' decimal currency, supported by allowances of two shillings and two pence for boots and a shilling for lamp oil, all to be paid monthly. However, out of this he would have to pay two thirds of the rent for his police accommodation but overall George was still much better paid compared with those in unskilled work such as agricultural workers who would form a significant part of his Beat in the years to follow. His first posting was to fill a vacancy at the time, being stationed in the singlemen's quarters at Southend-on-Sea Police Station, Essex with his 'beat' covering nearby Westcliff, where he robustly carried out the duties required of him as a novice policeman. Here, in this (especially at weekends) 'rough and ready' Thames estuary environment, he learnt the 'ropes' of the job and did not suffer fools lightly as those, such as street sellers and beggars were to find out in 'crossing' PC George Gutteridge, whose growing tenacity and

The Police Instruction Manual issued to George.
G.W. Gutteridge is written in his own hand on the inside cover.

Courtesy of the Essex Police Museum, Chelmsford

sometimes 'overly robust'! approach as a policeman was being noticed by his superiors and was beginning to show results. Six and a half months later he was given a new posting to Romford, 25 miles away in the east of the county.

George seated in the third row 1st from left

Courtesy of the Essex Police Museum, Chelmsford

The old Romford Police Station

The Old Romford Police Station, South Street in 1963. It was demolished soon after these pictures were taken. A new station was eventually built.

Courtesy, Havering Library Local studies

The Romford Police Force in 1910.
Taken before George arrived on the 19th December of that year.

Courtesy of Havering- Libraries Local Studies

However for George it frustratingly meant being another 25 miles away from his sweetheart Rose and no doubt a little 'put out' that his courtship should be so rudely interrupted again! But a close colleague and subsequent long-time friend at the Southend section house, PC George 'Tot' Totterdell realised that Bill Gutteridge was having to do a lot of travelling back and forth from Romford to Westcliff to see Rose and very kindly offered to share his bunk on occasion with Bill, an act of comradeship and to save his 'rookie' colleague a bit of money in those lean years.

George Henry Totterdell as PC 173 in 1913.
By kind permission of the family of G.H.R. Totterdell

George's service record shows that a few weeks into his posting to Romford he was disciplined for playing cards into the early hours of the morning with his section house colleagues; this being compounded by having left the gas lamp burning in his bedroom! As a result, the whole group were put on 'report' by Sergeant Philip

Davis for 'gambling cards in the single men's quarters at 3.15 am and wilfully wasting the gas.'

George, as several of his colleagues were given the option to do, gave a written response to this offence with George simply stating without offering any excuse that he had gone off duty at 10pm and wasn't due back on duty until 10am the next morning, being constantly aware of the time, as there was a clock on the wall in the room in which they were playing cards. George wrote; 'This is the first occasion that we have all been together playing cards and thought there was no harm in staying up so late'.

A perfectly honest response from a young man just socialising with his friends and in the same vein as the response he gave to a disciplinary form in years hence in failing to set his alarm clock correctly and missing a conference point which was also entered into his service record.

CHAPTER 3

ANOTHER MOVE AND A POSTING TO GRAYS

Grays police station as George Gutteridge would have known it.
It was rebuilt in 1930

Courtesy of gallery.nen.gov.uk

On the 22nd December 1911 he received another posting, this time to Grays, close to Tilbury and the bustling Thames estuary district of coastal Essex. Arguably this was to challenge George in many ways as he now faced policing in an environment very alien to his Norfolk country town roots where it was devoid of the hustle and bustle and urgency of the cosmopolitan and multi-cultural circus of very different lifestyle values and social mobility which he was now about to encounter. As a Norfolk man George was used to people (apart from the usual rogues in any village or town) in the main, observing the values of common decency, support for others and for the rule of the law illustrated in the form of the village 'Bobby' who by his presence, commanded respect by those on his 'beat' but was approachable and tactful in settling small disputes and often within his brief, willing to help those less able he saw as his responsibility. Almost in the context of a 'social worker' as he was famed for at his last posting in Stapleford Abbotts where he made the effort to know as much as possible about the indigenous population of his 'manor' which he logically considered would make it easier to police. 'Knowledge is power' as it is said.

For George, willing to exercise his usual level of zeal and dedication to his role as an Essex policeman in the sprawl of the dockland areas of Grays, Tilbury and nearby Kent, where marine traffic from all over the globe arrived to deposit their numerous forms of cargo for distribution primarily to London and eventually to the far corners of the United Kingdom, there now came a large number of equally diverse, multicultural and cosmopolitan merchant seamen. The illicit trade of 'black market' merchandise in these dockland areas at a time of political tension was rife with many in the local community actively taking part in clandestine deals in parallel with their legitimate activities. But sometimes the 'fallout' from those involved in 'dealings and transactions' resulted in disputes degenerating into violence between gangs and underworld individuals who had 'scores' to settle which, sometimes fuelled by drink, would escalate into disproportionate levels of conflict involving the use of knives, guns and other weaponry. (One of the Webley revolvers in Browne's possession was bought, he said after his arrest, from a sailor in this area.)

As can be appreciated, foreign merchant seamen and a proportion of some English ones in addition to some members of the indigenous local population, had little regard for life and limb or indeed, British law. As once back at sea it would be hard to apprehend those who had broken English law now out of British waters and legal jurisdiction. In later and more tragic times Bishop Inskip would question of George's murderers at the funeral, 'Are these indeed Englishmen?' Making, it seems, a reference to the growing levels of volence and disregard for the sanctity of life demonstrated by a small number of the increasingly international populus, so alien to the values of English conduct in Edwardian society.

However, the situation was to worsen and place much higher pressures on the already stretched Essex County Constabulary. To compound this further, union disputes and strikes were to escalate into major civil unrest; a dangerous flashpoint had been reached resulting from a decision made by the Port of London Authority to employ non-union workers and as Dr. Chipperfield explains; 'By early July of 1912 there were running battles between strikers and 'blacklegs' with only 450 officers in the whole county.'

Captain E. M. Showers, the Chief Constable had little choice but to request reinforcements from nearby forces in an attempt to contain the now increasingly volatile situation before it ran out of control but this was not enough. The situation continually worsened until the Grays Public Officers formally requested military assistance to restore order and to end this explosive, anarchistic stand-off between the warring factions of strikers, non-union workers with the police in the middle doing their utmost to keep them apart and maintain order. George, of course, certainly did not shirk his duty excercising the 'zeal' he was famous for and to the best of his ability as did his colleagues, but research shows that he did not wish to advance his police career in this turbulent environment in this part of Essex. Some other officers were awarded bonuses for duties which went beyond the call of duty but for George this type of policing probably challenged his expectations of the job and it is perfectly understandable that these experiences may have been a 'game changer' for him whose innate strength, ability and flair would flower in the rural environment; a mindset to which he was familiar and which would prove to be his forte in the dedication and bravery he demonstrated in going beyond the call of duty in the early morning of the 27th September 1927.

CHAPTER 4

TROUBLE AT THE GRAYS SECTION HOUSE AND ANOTHER MOVE FOR GEORGE

A further move was on the horizon due to an ongoing personality clash between George and the section housekeeper Mrs Jopson without any apparent sign of reconciliation. Mrs Jopson took great exception to comments straight-talking George made about her cooking and his attitude toward her. It was becoming increasingly obvious to all concerned that the situation was 'coming to a head' with frustration and tension rising on both sides, this becoming almost a daily occurrence. This reached the attention of the section house commander in the form of a letter of resignation from Mrs Jopson (original copy at Essex Police Museum) who in her lengthy letter of reluctant resignation was quite explicit in her criticism of George who, she went on to add, was also unpopular with his comrades at the section house (research does not corroborate this). She was well respected and considered a hard person to replace. This development caused quite a stir with one of the other constables at the Grays Police Station section house, PC Luckmore, who composed and sent the following letter to Superintendent Laver:

Sir,

I have the honour to report, that Mrs Jopson, who has been housekeeper in the single mens quarters here for some months past has given her notice to leave and as she has given every satisfaction and appears to like her situation, I asked her the reason for giving notice. When she told me she should be sorry to leave, and did not like giving notice but owing to the conduct of PC 489 Gutteridge in the absence of the other men, she felt compelled to do it she said he was always complaining of the way his food was prepared and that he was not clean in his habits. All the other men have said they should be very sorry to lose Mrs Jopson.

I might add that PC 489 Gutteridge has quarrelled with all the other men that are in the station now, and his conduct is generally unsatisfactory.

Original letter (with some punctuation amendment).

This tense situation needed to be considered and resolved. Superintendent Laver explained to his superior Captain Showers that removing this 'quarrelsome' officer would provide the best option as 'it is difficult to get a woman to suit the office of looking after the singlemen'.

Dr J. Chipperfield illustrates how the war had radically changed the social landscape with women now enjoying greater choice to say nothing of strengthening of the cause in achieving women's emancipation.

In this she states; 'It wasn't until after the first world war that the "servant problem" became truly pressing as women found better jobs in department stores, tea rooms, schools and city offices, and the doors to the professions and the universities began to crack open to them.'

Captain Showers considered the situation and took Superintendant Laver's advice with George being posted to Little Thurrock (detachment) Police Station, a short distance away in the singlemen's quarters to continue his duties as a beat Constable and for George it seemed he had probably reached a crossroads both in his career

George in uniform standing, second from left at Grays section house in 1912 with the formidable-looking Mrs Jopson seated at the centre of this picture.

Courtesy of the Essex Police Museum, Chelmsford

and his life and was clearly unhappy. If we reflect on George's life up to this point there is no previous hard evidence of the anti-social behaviours that George had *allegedly* displayed according to Mrs Jopson or PC Luckmore in their letters to Superintendent Laver. Indeed in other environments i.e. his very varied work with a range of former employers including the Reverend Samuel Howard as a child, a thread of honesty and a willingness to get along and socialise with others was a fundamental and an innate part of his character but George did not suffer fools lightly.

It seems quite obvious that, if true, the allegations made against him by Mrs Jopson and PC Luckmore were an understandable reaction to the type of policing he was faced with and the attendant stresses he was unused to. But it begs the question; was George 'difficult' from the time he arrived at Grays or were these isolated occurrences growing in intensity? If so, why was this not previously noticed and addressed by George's superiors to avoid further tensions which resulted in the ultimatum given by Mrs Jopson?

Indeed, in the aftermath of George's murder on the 29th September 1927, Sir Fielding Clarke, the Chairman of Grays Police Court was quoted as saying that, 'before the business of the court commenced, he wished, on behalf of the bench, to express their united and sincere sorrow and sympathy at the tragic death of PC Gutteridge. "He was well known there [at Grays] where he served faithfully and well, he believed for a period of about seven years. He was a young officer of great promise, with the best of character and with no doubt a most honourable and useful career before him".'

Superintendent Phillip Brown, on behalf of the Chief Constable thanked the chairman for his kind words being followed by Mr T. A. Capron, the Clerk of the Court going on to support the commendation of PC Gutteridge in saying that, 'I have come into contact with PC Gutteridge for about seven years and always found him a very faithful officer'. Courtesy of the *Essex Times*, Saturday October 1st 1927.

Arguably, the above commendations are in stark contrast to the subjective allegations made against him at Grays section house and there seems here to be a strong 'cry for help' here with growing dissatisfaction with his surroundings. George needed more consistency and stability and to put his roots down as a family man to work in an environment he felt comfortable in. He must have considered his situation very carefully; it is clear he was becoming unhappy and unsettled being shoved around from pillar to post away from his friends, further from Rose and continually having to re-adjust to the changing environment he was required to police, arguably the right policeman placed in the wrong environment.

The winds of change were now blowing, signalling a new phase in both his life and career and now George wanted to change things for the better and achieve his goal of marrying Rose. He was aware that if he was granted permission, this would be much more beneficial for Rose and himself including the award of a pay increase, the opportunity to apply for a village beat and no longer having to live in urban singlemen's quarters. This made sense for George and he had made his decision!

Before George could marry Rose, permission from the police authorities had to be granted. On the 28th July 1913 George composed and wrote a neat and well spelt letter of request to his superior, Superintendent Laver at Police HQ., Chelmsford. George and Rose must have made tentative enquiries with the vicar of Isleham, the Reverend Wilson Robinson in Fordham to establish a provisional date for their marriage, so after sending the letter below to his superiors I suspect George and Rose may have been holding their breaths to some extent as police procedural criteria had yet to be met!

In the interim, satisfactory character references had also to be sought for Rose, her family and her place of employment before permission to marry would be granted as, should there have been negative issues surrounding the respectability and character of Rose, her family or record of employment (see letter below), marriage may have been deemed unsuitable.

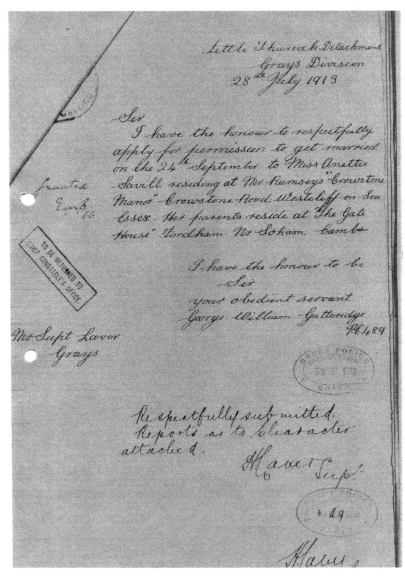

George's *original letter*, courtesy of the Essex Police Museum, Chelmsford.

(Note: It is interesting to see how George has not used his fiancé's first name Rose, rather referring to her as 'Annettie' or 'Nettie' as she was known by her family as pointed out by Brian Alexander.)

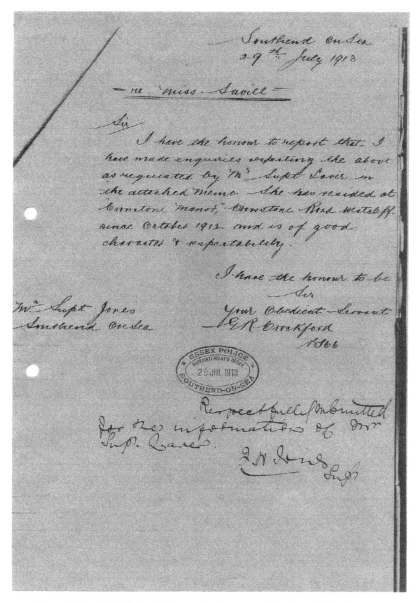

Southend on Sea
29th July 1913

— re 'miss Savill —

Sir,

I have the honour to report that I have made enquiries respecting the above as requested by Mr Supt Savir in the attached memo. She has resided at "Crowstone Manor," Crowstone Road Westcliff since October 1912 and is of good character & respectability.

I have the honour to be
Sir
your Obedient Servant
E R Crockford
1866

Mr Supt Jones
Southend on Sea

Respectfully submitted for the information of Mr Supt Lane.

A Copy of the original letter held at and by Courtesy of the Essex Police Museum, Chelmsford

Supt. Laver contacted Supt. Winter of Cambridgeshire Constabulary at nearby Newmarket, (who incidentally, had known the Savill family for some time), to request a character reference for Rose. He conducted this request promptly and by the next day, the 29th July, he had telegraphed his findings to Supt. Laver at Grays Police Station stating that;

'I have known the father of Miss Savill for about 7 years and I know nothing prejudicial to his character or that of his daughter'. But in this letter he states that he felt duty bound to mention one thing and he writes:

'I think I should inform you that his daughter Christina,was, on 4th December 1907 found decapitated on the railway and the coroner's jury returned a verdict "that the deceased committed suicide whilst being of unsound mind".'

The *Cambridge Independent News* the following day reported the jury verdict less diplomatically as: 'that the deceased committed suicide during temporary insanity'.

Concurrent with this, Supt. Laver directed Inspector John Crockford to conduct further enquiries about Rose to her employer Mr Rumsey at Crowstone Manor where she was in service also reporting back by telegraph on the 29th July that, 'she has resided at Crowstone Manor, Crowstone Road Westcliff since October 1912 and is of good character and respectability'.

The couple could now 'breathe out' and excitedly wait for the 24th of September 1913 to arrive; their wedding day.

George and Rose celebrated their marriage on the date requested at the lovely church of St. Peter and St. Mary Magdalene, Fordham in a double wedding in tandem with Rose's sister 'Minnie' May Irene and George Meadows, also a policeman and serving at Southend, both of whom played a supportive role to Rose in the aftermath of George 's murder, to be explained later. This happy dual family event was witnessed by Rose's father Alfred Savill but tinged with a little sadness in the absence of his late wife Sarah and probably compounded by the grief he must have still endured after the death of Christina. The presence of his other daughter Violet, who accompanied him must have given him huge support on this happy day. He must have been proud to 'give away' two of his daughters into the safe keeping of two police constables in the knowledge that they would enjoy a comparatively good standard of living and higher social standard as Mr and Mrs George Gutteridge and Mr and Mrs George Meadows.

George continued his period of duty at Little Thurrock detachment where he now resided with Rose in a two-up two-down terraced police house in relatively more comfortable married quarters at 2, Southend Road, on the corner with College Avenue, Grays. George was now relaxing into his comfort zone with his new wife 'Annettie', a more settled beat Constable working a discretionary five hour beat duty during the day with variably timed three hour night patrol duties. However, all constables including George remained 'on -call' at all times as the country remained in a state of emergency with dockland and major coastal inlets being patrolled 24 hours a day to guard against any attempt by enemy forces or agents to breach national security and commit bombings or as the authorities put it, 'outrages'.

The marriage of George and Rose was blessed two years later with the arrival of a lovely daughter Muriel, on the 7th December 1915, a year and a half after the onslaught of World War 1 had begun and early photographs depict how proud they were of her, especially the well-known and classic image of George sitting and looking fondly at his little girl standing beside him high on a stool.

(Date unknown and pictured below.)

No doubt George's grandfather who had died aged 80 in the April of 1915 would have been very proud to have seen his great

George pictured with Muriel.

Picture Courtesy, Mr Brian Alexander

granddaughter Muriel had he have lived, although by this time family communication may have dwindled possibly due to the restrictions of the war and it is unclear whether he saw her or was aware of her birth. This special and original posed photograph was kindly shown to me by the Alexander family in addition to other family photographs depicting an ordinary loving family at leisure with one showing George at the seaside and smiling with his family. I feel very privileged to have been privy to these wonderful images presented to me enclosed between the pages of a fragile and very old cherished family album which has never entered the public domain.

Despite many images depicting George as very stern and unsmiling, I have it on good authority that 'off duty' and away from the 'official camera', in company he demonstrated a very good sense of Norfolk-inspired humour, joked and smiled frequently. In the days following the birth of Muriel, George re-enlisted in the army reserve alongside his police career with the rank of Corporal with a very welcome extra weekly wage of three shillings and sixpence but in 1916 another one shilling and twopence came his way as a grant for his little daughter Muriel. This was issued to married constables who had children under 14 years old and was payable for each child. But despite having received an inflation-linked war bonus of two shillings per week George still needed to earn more money to keep up with the staggering rate of inflation which was sending prices through the roof at a rate of 27 per cent per annum. As a policeman, George was paid a set wage as a Constable regardless of how many extra hours he worked and the impact of inflation was illustrated further by Dr Chipperfield: 'Unlike the workers in industry, agriculture and commerce, policemen didn't receive any bonuses to compensate for either their increased working hours or crippling inflation'.

But by the summer of 1917, ever resourceful George, with a wife and two-year-old daughter, needed to supplement his income by working for Mr J. Ellingford, a farmer in nearby Orsett, Essex during his annual holidays; work he would have been very familiar with. George had made (as required) an official request to his superiors for permission to do this which was granted without reservation. Possibly there were two sides to this coin in that his superiors may have seen this request as Bill using his initiative in helping with the agricultural labour shortage caused directly by the still raging pointless war in Europe and other parts of the world but also to keep his 'head above water' financially because again as research shows 'he was lucky; police officers were liable to dismissal for getting into debt and failing to live "respectably".'

At the time Bill was also still supporting his mother on an ad-hoc basis and one could speculate that in supplementing his income in this way that a small part of this extra income may have found its way to Mary Edwards much to the annoyance of Rose, a sensitive issue which did cause arguments in the years to follow and may have, one could speculate, at that time too.

George, Rose and Muriel

Courtesy of Mr Brian Alexander and the Essex Police Museum

CHAPTER 5

CONSCRIPTION AND ARMY LIFE

But in mid–1918 as the Great War was entering it's last year and the world was reeling and counting the cost of needless, unimaginable human loss and social upheaval, George, now aged 28, received his 'call-up' papers. On the 30th April 1918 he compulsorily resigned from the Essex County Constabulary to join the army; enlisting in the 85th Training Reserve Battalion but by August 1918 he had been sent to the 4th Battallion Machine Gun Battallion, formed on the 26th February 1918 when the army was re-organised, to train as a gunner at the Clipstone Military Training Camp near Mansfield in North Nottinghamshire.

Cap Badge of the Great War Machine Gun Corps.

Courtesy of the Machine Gun Corps

As if Rose didn't have enough to worry about in looking after three-year-old Muriel and making ends meet, she would, as news of the terrible battles being fought (and lost) were posted daily including lists of those 'missing' or killed, have been acutely aware of the reports of carnage, heavy loss of life and with it the predictably low life expectancy of those men from all regiments, walks of life, social status, ability and occupation including royalty who were called to fight, gallantly facing the enemy with typical English patriotic fervour. This evaporated as they were faced with the reality of seeing their friends and comrades shot, gassed, picked off by snipers and blown to bits by shells before their eyes, now questioning with sinking morale, the whole purpose of this terrible war coupled with feelings of betrayal by their leaders such as General Haig, the phrase being coined, 'lions were being led by donkeys'

Although the government propaganda machine attempted to play this down, Rose, like the millions of other wives and mothers read between the lines of the hollow morale boosts, inaccurate tales of military successes they were being fed by newspapers and the predictable 'fire and brimstone' speeches given by politicians, they watched and listened with horror and sinking hearts; feeling betrayed and marginalised by those they trusted in their continual state of anxiety and worry.

Her new husband George may now have to face the 'Hun' as did millions of other men without choice but the skills George possessed as an army reservist and policeman were utilised at Clipstone and arguably could have saved his life, and the horrors of trench warfare. Rose now had joined the millions of other women whose lives were 'on hold' and dreaded the sight of the postman as he delivered letters and other mail down their streets with news for better or worse. Or, horror of horrors, the telegraph man knocking on their doors striking fear and foreboding in their thumping hearts as he handed them the small brown envelope.

Clipstone Military Training Camp Mansfield was built by an army of workers and finished in 1915 to train Lord Kitchener's new army of volunteers; known widely as 'Kitchener's Mob'. Clipstone Camp could accommodate up to 30,000 men and was considered to be the largest military training camp in the country.

Here, conscripts and volunteers alike were trained in a short and inadequate space of time to fight in the terrible battles to come, beginning with the Battle of Loos in 1915 but most notably the Battle of the Somme in 1916 (the same year conscription was introduced), where 20,000 British troops, to say nothing of similar numbers of German casualties, were killed on the first day of fighting; or should I say unmitigated slaughter, and the muddy, bloody hell of the Third Battle of Ypres known as Passchendaele, in Belgium from July to November 1917 where history laments the heavy losses suffered on both sides.

Images of Clipstone Camp by kind permission of The Forest Town Heritage Group

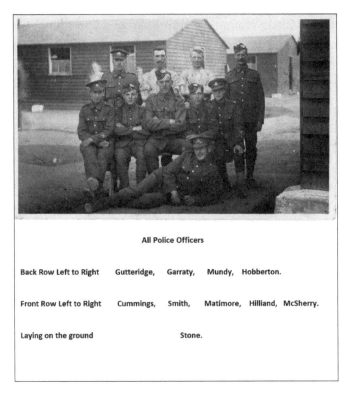

All Police Officers

Back Row Left to Right   Gutteridge,   Garraty,   Mundy, Hobberton.

Front Row Left to Right   Cummings,   Smith,   Matimore, Hilliand, McSherry.

Laying on the ground   Stone.

George and his Police Colleagues Ready for
Recruit Training Duty in Uniform at Clipstone Camp
Courtesy of The EPM

Bill's home-based conscription at Clipstone was classed as a short service attestation period, his duties including assisting with the management and training of the many conscripts and volunteers who were still being called to serve in the battles yet to be fought, with the Germans still engaged in a big push to win the war. (His skills being more valuable at home than being posted abroad. But this was not 'set in stone' as WW1 military history often shows.) Here, George would join other regional policemen from a range of regiments (pictured above) who would be assigned to train new recruits in addition to their own specialist training and I would suggest that with the previous rank of Lance Corporal as a reservist in the Norfolk Regiment, George Gutteridge would not have been faced with a big culture shock with strict army discipline and drilling as his duties at Clipstone, it could be said, represented somewhat of a 'busman's holiday' to George and must have appealed to his streetwise and assertive nature in dealing with new recruits as opposed to those often very difficult individuals who had transgressed the law in his recent work as a policeman and certainly as a constable in the riotous Grays of recent years.

It is also worth observing that at a time of high patriotic fervor which for all able-bodied men demanded allegiance to King and Country, a man had to show his willingness and determination *publicly* to serve as a soldier for fear of the social stigma of being accused of cowardice or avoidance to pick up a rifle and fight for his country. Conscientious objectors as we know were treated very harshly and their families ostracised never really being forgiven for their perceived cowardice even to this day. This 'blanket' call to duty at a time of war applied equally to serving policeman who were obliged to represent a positive and proud example of patriotic duty to their own police forces and to the communities to which they would return after serving conscripted military service. They would proudly resume their police duties with, arguably, a much greater credibility in having served their country adorned in rough government issue khaki in addition to the slightly better and more carefully tailored blue/black of a smart serge police uniform.

At the close of World War One with a nation celebrating victory over the Kaiser's brutal attempts at world dominance, those brave soldiers who were left of Kitchener's 'New' Army were demobilised and were returned to their towns and villages, many as broken men and old before their time; unable to live and work as they did before the war having suffered irreparable physical and psychological damage such as shell shock and post traumatic stress disorder, a condition existent but not fully recognised medically until many years later.

Those who did return, did their best to pick up the reins of life and work in the same way as they had before they went to war but now faced new social and economic challenges in their home towns and villages which had now changed forever.

Clipstone Camp was gradually being de-commissioned and with a skeleton staff in the role of caretakers, this huge training camp had served its grim patriotic purpose and faced closure.

The camp became less and less used for training soldiers and alternative uses, eventually being dismantled in sections with the large wooden buildings being sold off as sheds, for agricultural, community and many other uses including village halls.

To Roses's relief, George was demobilised and re-enlisted as Police Constable Gutteridge 218 in the Essex County Constabulary; returning to his wife and daughter to his Little Thurrock (detachment) base on the 23$^{rd.}$ February 1919 a matter of only months before the surrender of Germany and the end of the First World War. His police number had changed from PC 489 to PC 218 as when he was conscripted, this obliged him to resign as a serving policeman. Upon re-enlistment he was issued with a new number, his previous number being allocated to another policeman. Soon after the Great War, the Prime Minister Lloyd George promised many changes in his new vision of a 'country fit for heroes to live in' with enhanced pension and unemployment benefits including, amongst others, a long-overdue review of police pay and conditions conducted by Lord Desborough.

The appointed committee reprted that huge inequalities existed between urban and rural police forces and indeed between different county constabularies.

The changes that were implemented resulting from the Desborough enquiry were very favourable for police officers who would now be eligible for a pension after having served 25 years instead of the previous 30, police widows would be awarded 10 shillings per week as poor Rose was to sadly find out, child benefits would increase and serving officers could now live in police accommodation rent free but on top of this Lord Desborough directed that every serving officer should immediately be given a payment of £10!

I expect there must have been much celebration in the Gutteridge household.

It used to be said that 'a policeman's lot is not a happy one' and in view of George's experiences on the front lines of the civil disturbances, strikes, blockaded policemen and running battles in 1912 Grays, nothing had changed. These extreme experiences understandably must have challenged George's expectations of police work and he, like most officers had to be continually vigilant against verbal and physical attack from those who had little regard for the law and for those who represented it, namely policemen. This was well illustrated on the 11th September 1920 whilst George was on duty at Little Thurrock in Grays, when, in the process of arresting a thief he was assaulted by another man who punched him in the face. Both men were arrested and taken into custody. Mr G. M. Page the Deputy Chief Constable reported on the outcome to the Chief Constable in a letter Dated the 18th September 1920. It read:

Assault on PC 218 Gutteridge

I have to report that at the Grays petty sessions on the 17th September 1920 William Daley of Leyton was fined £2 for assaulting PC Gutteridge while in the execution of his duty at Grays on the 11th instant by striking in the face with his fist while arresting a man named Allen for larceny.

GM Page, Deputy Chief Constable

I would hazard a guess that Bill dealt with these two men in a very robust way!

CHAPTER 6

BILL RETURNS TO WHERE HIS HEART LAY, THE COUNTRYSIDE

It always has to be remembered that Bill Gutteridge was born and raised in the Norfolk village of Wimbotsham, a stone's throw from the wide open, flat and sparsely populated Norfolk and Cambridgeshire fens where he worked hard mainly in the building trade until joining the police force in April 1910. Southend, Grays and the Thames estuary districts must have been quite a culture shock for Bill who would be subsequently faced with criminal behaviour being committed on a very regular basis by a continual and uninterrupted flow of thefts, violence, daily disputes between dockers, unions and of course, some of the indigenous local population; a proportion of whom had no regard for the law unless there was a hidden agenda from which they would benefit.

Dr Chipperfield succinctly states that, 'All in all, George was better suited to the role of "Village Bobby" - it was a life he understood, moving at a pace he had been brought up with, and with very different concerns from the docks of East London'.

It seems that George was somehow drawn like a magnet to his real roots in the rural environment, maybe his superiors realised this (without admitting it) by not objecting to his farm work at Orsett? So when the opportunity arose to fill a vacancy in the small Essex village of Stapleford Abbotts, he applied for this (rather than be sent, raising George's sense of self-empowerment), as he could now take his wife and daughter and the policing style he aspired to, into an environment similar to the one he had originated from, a homecoming one could say, but with now a higher status socially, professionally and financially.

The Beautiful Rabbits Pub at Stapleford Abbotts

Pictures by author and by kind permission of the proprietors

George, Rose and little Muriel were housed in a very small former farmworker's cottage rented by the Essex County Constabulary adjoining Bons Farm situated a short distance downhill from the picturesque 'Rabbits' public house in the village of Stapleford Abbotts. Some of these cottages at Bons Farm, as do all of the 12 Towneley Cottages in Tysea Hill, still exist today but all are now in private ownership, understandably having been vastly 'individualised' to meet the requirements and needs of a range of owners over the years and modernised to meet today's living standards.

In later years, Muriel Alexander was to recall how basic the little two-up two-down cottage at Bons Farm was, without electricity or running water, a brick floor and very little heating only provided from an open fire in front of which stood a trivet (a small cast iron or brass stand) on which to cook their food. This scenario would probably have been familiar to George and possibly Rose but provided a useful insight and a reminder to some extent, of how very poor agricultural workers were at that time with wages varying between

28 to 46 shillings per week depending on length of service and role. George was now being paid £4 and 6 shillings per week.

In 1920 the coalition government attempted to establish minimum price guarantees for agricultural products and wages for farm workers through the ill-fated Agricultural Act of 1920, but as this was administered by county wage committees who then allowed wages to be set at local levels through agreement with local farmers and landowners rather than on a national scale, there was no legal redress should a farmer or landowner ignore the guidelines. The act essentially floundered and was doomed from the outset being abandoned in 1921. A further act of Parliament in 1924 suffered a similar fate and although wages rose slightly, it was not until 1948 that the Agricultural Wages Act replaced the previous acts of 1920 and '24. (Source: https://enwikipedia.org/windex.php?)

Home ownership was, of course, out of the question for rural and unskilled workers until some years later with agricultural workers being entirely reliant upon a 'tied' cottage owned by the farmer or landowner, their accommodation having virtually no security of tenancy and only being allowed to live there during their period of employment or in special cases, at the discretion of the landlord. This was equally the case with rented county police houses as Rose Gutteridge was to experience in a very harsh way after George's murder in the lean 1920s following the Great War and the outbreak of the pandemic 'Spanish flu' which infected 500 million, eventually claiming more lives worldwide (between an estimated 50 to 100 million), than the Great War itself.

Many agricultural and other communities found themselves still reeling from the effects of war, disease and the loss or disablement of brave working men who would never return to their villages and towns so they did what they could to survive in the void left by young men sent to their deaths in France Belgium and other theatres of war in this climate of social and financial depression with inflation running into three figures. George, Rose and Muriel had to make the best of what facilities and living arrangements they had been provided with by the Essex County Constabulary and no doubt George, using the skills he had acquired in his previous wide ranging employment in the building trade made sure his new family was as comfortable as they could be in the circumstances, while still carrying out his duties as the village policeman.

'Bill', as he was known in the village was a very confident 'people person' who made sure he gained a good perspective and knowledge of the local population; good and not so good, by integrating himself socially mostly at the 'Rabbits' and latterly the Royal Oak (known then, as today by the locals and recently being renamed the 'Top Oak'), where he took full part in having a few pints and as was well known, sometimes having more than a few! These pubs gave George the opportunity to socialise with the people he had to police and as such he 'connected' with the local grapevine gaining whispers of any planned dark deeds such as horse rustling, theft or poaching activities and more compassionately, offering a listening ear to those with concerns or problems in this relatively small Essex village he had made his own.

However, his style of policing and 'undercover' poaching activities would no doubt have raised a few eyebrows amongst his superiors in those times and would have attracted instant disciplinary action or dismissal if he had been caught.

As an example of Bill's own 'disturbance control' methods, should a fight break out in one of these pubs as they occasionally did, George, also very handy with his fists and who regularly took part in section house bouts whilst at Grays, (pictured), would, I am reliably informed, put his coat behind the bar, join in the battle and settle things between the warring factions rather than arrest all involved creating a large amount of paperwork for himself which, I am sure with his apparently limited amount of compulsory elementary education, he would have gone to some lengths to avoid!

George pictured second from left with PC Sydney Taylor on the far right looking rather serious in talking to a local

A picture of George, second from left taking his turn with colleagues as a 'second' during boxing practice at Grays Section House. EPM

Bill Gutteridge fitted like a hand in a glove with this approach to his work in this essentially farmworking community and post Victorian and Edwardian policing methods, and although changing, attacks on policemen were common and still endured in those days.

It could be said that George's personal and physical qualities were a great advantage, in an essentially agricultural community where issues and 'storms in teacups' had to be dealt with quickly and were not for the 'faint hearted'.

George, I would suggest, would have been very aware as a former hard working labourer that a man may lose his job, possibly his house and expose his family to hardship should he suddenly have to face the consequences of his actions in court and possibly gain a criminal record for fighting, being drunk and disorderly etc. I believe that his community knew this and respected his way of protecting them even if they found themselves on the receiving end of his style of policing as research shows that Bill Gutteridge was no 'pushover'.

Probably one of George's most valuable assets was that he had a natural presence and charisma which to some extent demanded respect as the face of the law in his community and someone who did not suffer fools lightly. However, research illustrates a village policeman and family man with a firm but fair approach and an innate 'sixth sense' in sniffing out criminal activity. I would suggest that the level of severity he used with lawbreakers would be dependent on those he was dealing with at any given time or situation.

Bill's 'down to earth' policing methods within this small agricultural community he took under his wing and accepted full responsibility for, awarded him a credibility and respect which remained intact throughout his time in Stapleford Abbotts and is still very much in existence today in the minds of existing residents and those who may have known him, albeit they would be very old now or long term residents having being told of his tragic story and to quote the late 'Titch' Dolman, 'there wasn't a boy or girl that didn't respect him right down to his boots'.

On the 29th April 1923 at 7pm, Mr Stallard of Chadwell Heath had paid a visit to a field at Crown Park Farm owned by a well-known local dairy farmer Mr Charlie Binder to check on his and other horses which were grazing in a paddock. He left, satisfied that the horses were there and grazing peacefully with all seemingly being well. But later that evening at around 11.30pm and quite by chance, as he and some friends were driving near Loxford Bridge in Barking, Mr Stallard spotted three men leading two horses along the road in the dark who were suddenly illuminated in the headlamps of his approaching car. Recognising one of the horses as his own which he last saw grazing earlier on in the evening with the other which he also recognised as belonging to Mr Binder, he abruptly stopped the car. Mr Stallard and his son leapt out and strode towards the three men who ran off, leaving the horses (one with a bridle still attached) to be caught by Mr Stallard and his son, and later returned to their field at Crown Park Farm, Stapleford Abbotts. The bridle used in the theft was now evidence and would prove to be the undoing of these horse thieves.

Mr Stallard and Mr Binder reported this incident to Bill Gutteridge who, the next day accompanied by PC Sydney Taylor, were given permission to pursue this crime into the Metropolitan Police district. On the 5th May, Bill's zeal and tenacity with the assistance of PC Taylor got the result they were after, apprehending three young labourers; 19-year-old Daniel Cunningham, 18-year-old Daniel King and 16-year-old Edward Gray all from the Barking area. As the thieves were spotted at night and ran off quickly to escape, Mr Stallard was unable to give police an accurate description of the men but after four days of extensive enquiries, PCs Bill Gutteridge and Sydney Taylor made an early morning visit at 6.30am to the very surprised Daniel Gray as he lay in bed who admitted being the owner of the bridle. Not wishing to take the punishment for the whole escapade, Daniel Gray named his accomplices and they were eventually arrested.

Appearing at Essex Quarter Sessions on the 20th June 1923, the trio had little choice but to plead guilty for their crime and were sent to Borstal, for three years each. The work of PCs Bill Gutteridge and Sydney Taylor did not go unnoticed with the following memo being sent to Superintendent Ellis by Capt. Unett, the Chief Constable:

To Spt. Ellis.

P.C.s 218 Gutteridge and 119 Taylor are commended by the Chief Constable for their perseverance and tact in arresting 3 youths for stealing 2 horses from a field at Stapleford Abbotts on the 29th April, 1923.

These commendations were entered and appear in their records of service.

CHAPTER 7

A NEW ARRIVAL FOR BILL AND ROSE

Their cramped little dwelling at Bons Farm seemed to become a little more 'smaller' with the arrival on the 19th September 1923 of Alfred John who was affectionately known by friends and family throughout his life as 'Jack'. Two years later, the little cottage at Bons Farm was returned to farm worker accommodation as the Essex County Constabulary had now rented No.2 Towneley Cottages in Tysea Hill, Stapleford Abbotts for county police use.

The original cast iron sign at Towneley Cottages as it is today.

Photo by Author

Towneley Cottages circa. 1927. No.2 is the second in from the left and would wear the plaque of the 'County Police' when George was stationed there.

Courtesy of the late John Alexander and Stapleford Abbotts Historical Society

The beautifully landscaped rear of 2, Towneley Cottages as it is today.

By kind permission of Mrs Elizabeth Coon.
Picture by author

The established and very long garden at the rear of 2, Towneley Cottages as it is now.

By kind permission of Mrs E Coon.

Picture by author

This cottage would now be the new and more strategic central location for the village policeman with the Gutteridge family, relocating to this new home in early February 1925. The former occupant of this lovely cottage was Archibald John Wade a gifted scholar and aspiring Army Chaplain with the 8th Somerset Light Infantry in World War One. Again, this terrible conflict claimed another life when 'Archie', as he was known, was killed at the Battle of Cambrai on the 9th October 1918 tragically by his own artillery (known as 'short shelling') but as with many soldiers in that senseless and brutal war, his death elevated Archibald to hero status. His body was never found but his name is inscribed on panel 4 in the British cemetery at Vis-en-Artois near Arras in France.

No.2 Towneley Cottages would sadly be the bearer of a second hero in the years to come with the sad loss of PC George Gutteridge.

Stapleford Abbotts School in earlier times. Courtesy of Stapleford Abbotts Historical Society and the village Primary School

Stapleford Abbotts Primary School as it is today. The main building and especially the large classroom at the front with arched window, having been lovingly restored over time with great care to maintain the original fabric and features including the original school bell in the playground!

Photo by author

The young Muriel Gutteridge (seated second on the left, 3rd row down) can be seen in the above faded class photograph at Stapleford Abbotts School. On close examination some of the children appear to be very poor sons and daughters of farm workers and children from the forest judging by their clothes. This was confirmed in later years by Muriel Alexander (nee Gutteridge).

Courtesy of Mr Brian Alexander and Stapleford Abbotts Primary School

Muriel, seated first left on the front row with her class and teacher.

Courtesy of Stapleford Abbotts Primary Scool and Mr Brian Alexander

For little Muriel, she was also to relocate from the village school in Stapleford Abbotts to the small council elementary school at Havering-Atte-Bower as it was now the nearest school to her new home. Muriel Gutteridge, (now Alexander), recalled in later years that seven classes were conducted in one room, a teacher would take the first and second year pupils with the Headmaster Mr Derrick teaching the third, fourth, fifth, sixth and seventh year pupils all at once with the adjoining room housing the infant class taken by his wife Mrs Derrick. George and Rose's new terraced police cottage in Tysea Hill was one of twelve built originally by the social reformer, philanthropist and humanitarian Lord O'Hagen and his second wife Alice, Lady O'Hagan (nee Towneley), whom he married in 1871, the daughter of Colonel Charles Towneley of Towneley Park Burnley, Lancashire.

After her father died, Lady O'Hagan inherited the Towneley estates. She subsequently gave a third of these to her new husband Thomas, Lord O'Hagan who had now essentially retired from public life after nearly 50 years of successful public service mainly in Ireland where he also became Lord Chancellor of Ireland. Prefferring now to live in England, they adopted the stately Pyrgo Palace to the east of Havering originally bought by Henry VIII (one of several beautiful large palaces in this area steeped in royal history including Bedfords Palace and Havering Palace now all sadly long gone), as their English country home. Here they set up a successful 'Towneley Institute' at Pyrgo Park, originally a reading room for their male staff to imrove their literacy and numeracy skills, a very forward thinking move by employers who were well aware that a better educated staff would be of benefit to all concerned and hopefully set an example to other employers of the effectiveness of 'in-house' education. Aways giving the welfare of their staff prominence, Lord and Lady O'Hagan went on to build two cottages in nearby Noak Hill for the use of their farm employees.

Very soon, they built upon the success of these and had twelve cottages constructed in Tysea Hill also for the welfare and use of their staff. Thomas O'Hagan, 1st Baron O'Hagan died in London in 1885 but was buried in Glasnevin Cemetery, Dublin in the country of his birth. The widowed Lady Alice O'Hagan found Towneley Park in Lancashire too expensive to maintain and subsequently sold the family home to Burnley Corporation. In 1901 and on the 20th November 1921, she died. They had both left a legacy of compassion for others which has survived the test of time.

The Rt. Hon. Lord O'Hagan KP PC QC in 1868
Author and copyright holder unknown but by kind courtesy of 'https://en.wikipedia.org/w/index.php?

In the years during and following the Great War a huge void of manpower in farming and many other occupations had been exposed, the male workforce having been decimated. Now, the cottage at No.2, formerly being occupied by, as previously explained, scholar and aspiring army chaplain Archibald Wade, killed without trace in the Great War had now become available and had been rented by the Essex County Constabulary to become a police house. Mrs Margaret Sutton informed me that all twelve Towneley Cottages were sold for £1000 at the time!

George, Rose and the children could now enjoy living in a very well built, sturdy, spacious and well-appointed cottage in stark comparison with the basic and harsh living conditions of the former police cottage at Bons Farm. No.2 Townelely Cottages boasted a *then* comparatively luxurious three bedrooms and two rooms downstairs, scullery and kitchen. It also had a large front garden with an even bigger garden to the rear of the cottage where George and Rose would establish a large kitchen garden as did most of the neighbours, providing food essentials such as potatoes and other vegetables to supplement their income. George's first grandson Mr Brian Alexander recalled to me that the gardens did not have fences between them and were essentially 'open' almost like allotments, where people respected each other's space; helping each other out as the need arose and interestingly, Mr Alexander went on to say that in addition to the outside toilet, coal shed etc, there was also a small but secure and sturdy building which could be used if necessary as a 'mini-jail' to hold people Bill had arrested whilst they were waiting to be transported to the cells at Romford or Epping police stations.

With the arrival of the Gutteridge family at Towneley Cottages and the establishment of a county police house in their midst, an element of resentment by some members of the immediate community became evident and grew almost from the beginning. Records show that an infirm old lady living next door at 1 Towneley Cottages Mrs Clarice Sutton, took great exception to Muriel Gutteridge and other children playing excitedly in their usual childlike way and running around up and down alleyways between the cottages together as a group. Mrs Sutton used to complain regularly about the antics of the children to Rose, and others about this, saying that 'Rose Gutteridge doesn't do anything to control her child, and they only behave when George is at home', going on to say that Muriel and the other children run around her house shouting 'eagle, eagle' considering that this name calling was directed at her. Was it a physical feature of this lady or did they simply feel that she was always watching them which prompted the children to call her this? We will probably never know for sure. I could speculate that if she was regarded as a complainer and constantly looking at what the children were doing, this could be an expected response from a group of lively and cheeky youngsters? Mrs Sutton's son Reuben a painter, wrote to Bill's superiors about the children's behaviour and alleged name-calling aimed at Mrs Sutton sending a letter which arrived at police headquarters on the 28th March 1927. Archived statements indicate that Reuben Sutton and his mother were apparently 'not popular with their neighbours' at Towneley Cottages as appears to be, in their view, in the original letter from Reuben Sutton:

'I am a painter and reside at Towneley Cottages. Last summer my mother spoke to PC Gutteridge and PC Gutteridge told my mother he had no intention of speaking to her (Muriel). We let the matter drop.

On Saturday last, I was going out with my bicycle. PC Gutteridge's child and other children were in the road and the Gutteridge girl said, 'Here come Monkey'. This is the only complaint I have to make about PC Gutteridge but all the people in the other eleven houses are against us. My chief complaint is that the children call my mother 'Eagle'.

(Signed.) L. Sutton

George was required to provide a report on the situation to his superiors which he did providing a detailed picture of life in the small community in which he lived and had paid his usual close attention to finding out who was who, what they did for a living and of course providing a good perspective of the ebb and flow of friendships, disputes and village gossip. This report is not just singularly valuable in providing an historical insight into this small area of Stapleford Abbotts during Bill's brief time there but more so as his report is almost devoid of the formality of police 'reporting grammar' possibly inhibited by the limited formal education he received as a child. But herein, one could almost be listening to his voice and the Norfolk dialect expressed in the way he writes.

The unedited and original report from George reads:

I beg to report re Mr Sutton's of Townley Cottages Stapleford Abbots letter of the 19th inst re my alleged conduct that Townley Cottages consist of a row of 12 cottages with a population of about 65 persons including about 20 school children and 15 others between 14 and 21 years. From the road to the back doors there is a 8ft rightaway to each of every three cottages, one for No1, 2 & 3, which passes along the gable end of No 1 & within a yard of its back door, (there is a pailing fence between the door and rightaway) the Suttonses family consists of the mother & grown-up son & daughter, at No. 3 there is two boys age 6 & 12 years & I have two children, a girl aged 11 and a boy 3 ½ years & they are playmates of No. 3

For the past 5 years of have known all the tenants of this row & previous to my living here there was frequent quarrels between the Suttons and others with families owing to Suttons interfering with children. On several occasions Suttons complained to me & me about the children & and their parents & upon enquiry I ascertained from childless people and others that there was no cause for complaint the Suttons being the aggressors … Not at any time have I had an argument or done anything to cause them annoyance. Nor has my wife & family. The Suttons has extraordinary views concerning all children & the use of our back rightaway by us and others, there is not hardly a sound in our house between 6pm and 7am each day. Unfortunately there is only a 4 ½ inch party wall between these cottages.

George made attempts to pour oil on troubled waters but due to the frequency of the complaints about the children, George eventually refused to speak to Reuben again about this. However, some members of this particular Sutton family apparently rejected offers of friendship from the Gutteridges and unfortunately the issues of children playing around and about the cottages and the bad feeling that existed between Clarice, Reuben and Bill was apparently never entirely resolved whilst Bill was alive.

Author's note

The name Sutton was also very familiar in this area but I am reliably informed that not all of these families are related. All accounts are factual and sourced from original files and letters held in the Gutteridge archives at the Essex Police Museum. My apologies for any unintentional offence caused to existing families by the name of Sutton in Stapleford Abbotts and the surrounding district.

Dissatisfied at having a policeman stationed in their midst, the gossip mongers of this small community, as there always seems to be some, turned their attention to Rose who quite innocently had accepted a lift in a car on several occasions from a male member of the neighbourhood who welcomed the presence of a policeman in his community and was supportive in helping Rose as an act of innocent friendship. This of course was 'noticed' and at remarkable speed reached the village 'grapevine' where through its distorted journey had been sensationalised and blown out of all proportion by those judgemental few watching from the part-drawn curtains and 'street watchers' whispering to each other, displaying mock horror on their faces.

This, of course, in some surreptitious way came to the notice of Inspector Poulton, George's superior who had little option but to look into the allegations being made against Rose Gutteridge. If they *were* true, it would have compromised George's position as village constable and made his position untenable exposing Rose to be a 'weak link' in the expected example of moral and law abiding fortitude a policeman and his family had to display for fear of being accused of hypocrisy and posessing double standards. 'We had to be perfect,' recalled Muriel Alexander speaking of her childhood as a policeman's daughter to Dr Maureen Scollan in November 1991. In his usual and thorough way, Inspector Percy Poulton made a series of enquires throughout the village, from those who had made the allegations, to others who liked having a policeman in their village and who felt safer as a result, including colleagues of George to arrive at a balanced and fair conclusion to the matter. This included PC Sydney Taylor who was stationed at Lambourne End and who was also one of George's colleagues, ironically the last policeman to see him alive.

PC Taylor told Inspector Poulton that he had heard stories from people in the community, together with other 'whispers' expressed by the less friendly element of the village which had cast, (and which proved to be unfounded), doubts on Rose's fidelity. Inspector Poulton met with Rose to see if there was any foundation to these rumours, but most importantly asked Rose to verify the loyalty she had with her husband and were there any problems within the marriage. Rose quietly explained that there had been some difficulties some four years previously due to George financially assisting his mother Mrs Edwards on an occasional basis as she (Mrs Edwards) used to send 'cadging' letters to George which would arrive at their home close to George's pay day. Rose explained that other than this, everything was alright.

Responding quietly and positively to the allegations of impropriety, Rose went on that explain to Inspector Poulton that she had received lifts from a man in the village who had a car but always had her daughter Muriel with her as it would save them walking to Havering Village, Romford and other places. It appears that Inspector Poulton had effectively used the 'lift issue' to establish whether Rose was being truthful after gathering much information before speaking to her.

The response Rose gave to Inspector Poulton was truthful and correct and, before their meeting, Poulton had already spoken to the local man and owner of the car together with other villagers who had positively stated that they saw Muriel with Rose on these short trips and that Rose never accepted lifts when she was on her own. Rose was therefore uncompromised and duly exonerated with the credibility of herself and her loyal husband and village policeman George, remaining firmly intact to the chagrin of the gossip mongering few.

In the late afternoon of Saturday the 3rd May 1924, local farmer Mr Arthur Viney reported to Bill Gutteridge that between Tuesday 29th April and Thursday 1st May he found that a lot of King Edward seed potatoes valued at ten shillings were missing from his barn at Standish Farm near to Tysea Hill and suspected that they had been stolen after asking some of his own employees if they knew anything about this.

Watercolour of Standish Farm in the 1920s by John Alexander.

Courtesy of Brian Alexander

Bill wrote in a report that 'he was satisfied that the potatoes were not now on the premises' and commenced his enquiries beginning with another local road worker David Dolman who had been seen in Arthur Viney's barn along with Thomas Sutton on the 29th April 'examining a sack of seed potatoes' but gave their reason for being there as 'sheltering from the rain'. Bill writes that;

> 'I am satisfied that "Dolman" did not steal these potatoes but strongly suspect Sutton who is a married man and is well known to be in financial difficulty. He also has an allotment which he has dug but not planted and admits he has neither no seeds or money to buy any.'

Bill expresses some frustration in the conclusion to his letter that, 'I am convinced that had Mr Viney reported his loss direct to the police instead of enquiring from off his workmen these potatoes would have been found in [Sutton's] possession'.

Bill obviously considered that Arthur Viney had inadvertently alerted the thieves by talking to his men first which in those very poor times could be interpreted as protecting his employees by giving them the chance to 'own up' without involving the police and possibly being prosecuted if found guilty. Bill's 'gut' instinct made him focus his enquiries on Thomas Sutton, who lived in the vicinity in a cottage at Martins Hearn farm in Tysea Hill. Bill understandably had strong suspicions about Thomas Sutton, driven by the information he had about this man's dire financial circumstances. Montagu 'Monty' William Martin of Mitchell's Farm at How Green was quoted as saying that 'Bill had a very inquisitive nature and went out of his way to find out as much as he could about people and their business in the community'. Bill now understandably suspected that as Thomas Sutton lived close by, stealing seed potatoes to grow on his own allotment and possibly to sell some for cash, may have eased his money worries.

A strong set of circumstantial evidence lay in front of him but Bill needed proof. Bill took Thomas Sutton to task over this but without corroborated proof or admittance by him, a charge could not be brought. Later in the week as Bill was on patrol of the neighbourhood with PC Cameron, his suspicions were raised further as they spotted an empty seed potato sack emblazoned with 'King Edward Potatoes' hanging from the old corrugated fence outside Thomas's cottage. Bill and his colleague decided to investigate further and knocked assertively on the front door. Thomas opened it to find Bill and PC Cameron standing there who asked him again about the seed potatoes which were being stolen from Arthur Viney's Farm; pointedly asking him if he knew anything about this which again, he vehemently denied. PC Cameron then pointed to the seed potato sack hanging on the fence and asked Thomas Sutton if it was his.

Thomas replied defiantly that it wasn't and he didn't know how it had got there but recently had used it by filling it with soot from his chimney and then had tipped it out on his allotment to help the plants grow. With suspicion rising, Bill Gutteridge was unconvinced by Thomas Sutton's answer asking him what type of potatoes he was growing on his allotment and that he would like to see where these were planted. Thomas reluctantly agreed to show Bill and PC Cameron the potato plot on his allotment but Bill noticed that the ground had been freshly dug over. Thomas said that he had planted some seed potatoes but these were not King Edwards as were suspected as the missing variety, but another strain known as 'Arram Chief'. Thomas offered to dig them up to show them to Bill and PC Cameron but they declined his offer.

Bill and his colleague left, but whenever Bill saw Thomas he continued to ask him about the missing potatoes but without result. Some days later whilst Thomas was visiting his mother at her Towneley Cottages home, Bill again arrived with his colleague, PC Cameron and asked Harvey to show him where the seed potatoes were kept at Viney's Farm telling Thomas that he had been seen by some 'very good people' carrying bags on his back, on his way up Tysea Hill to his cottage at Martin's Hearn Farm. By now, Thomas Sutton considered that Bill Gutteridge was harassing him and that an historic and deeper resentment was increasing between them.

They fetched David Dolman to accompany them with Thomas to the farm to look at the barn where the seed potatoes would be kept. On this occasion, Arthur Viney was working at the farm as the four arrived with Bill, carrying the empty King Edward seed potato sack which had been hanging on Thomas's fence explaining to Arthur Viney why they were there and saying that he strongly suspected that Thomas was responsible for stealing some of the missing King Edward seed potatoes, adding that he had heard that firewood was also being taken. Bill also asked Arthur Viney if the sack he had brought along matched the sort Arthur used, with Arthur confirming this.

Arthur Viney, being aware of Thomas's difficult personal circumstances told Bill that 'if Thomas had wanted some wood he would have given it to him if he had asked'.

Bill questioned Thomas again in front of Arthur Viney both about the stolen potatoes and wood and in growing frustration, Thomas asked Bill Gutteridge 'to bring forward the accusers' who had apparently reported that they had seen him carrying sacks up Tysea Hill. Bill remained silent and did not answer although his 'gut intuition' was still telling him that Thomas was responsible. This must have frustrated Bill as there was a distinct lack of corroborated evidence, which could not be proved. Bill subsequently visited Thomas again at his cottage asking about the potatoes, this time taking a different approach with the comment, 'I've been good to you Thomas', possibly overlooking other smaller offences George suspected Thomas may have been party to in the past, and attempting to temper the situation but to no avail, with Thomas still 'bristling' with resentment.

As he was leaving Thomas's cottage, Bill became aware that a neighbour had witnessed this disagreement which by now had become heated.

Walking away, Bill looked over his shoulder and said to Thomas 'not to be so bloody saucy in future', implying, in my view that he still thought that Thomas had taken the potatoes and was still watching his movements as a suspect and Thomas knew it. This incensed Thomas who told Bill he was 'fed up with this' and that he was going to write to Bill's superiors about his language with Bill retorting, 'You can write where you bloody well like.' Thomas Sutton made an official written complaint against Bill Gutteridge who was called to answer for his actions to Inspector Poulton.

The charge on his misconduct form dated the 8th May 1924 read:

'In that he, PC 218 Gutteridge at Stapleford Abbotts was uncivil to a member of the public using the following expressions towards him viz: "Not to be so bloody saucy" also, "you can write where you bloody well like".'

There were no consequences for Bill as the Chief Constable had dismissed the complaint through 'no corroboration of the charge'.

Police procedure of course, required that a misconduct form with all correspondence and witness statements had to be completed and entered into Bill's personal police file as an internal disciplinary record.

PC 518 Cameron had been asked to further investigate the issue of the stolen seed potatoes but in his report of the 10th May 1924 to Inspector Poulton, which was forwarded to Superintendent Ellis he concluded that; 'I beg to report that I have made enquiries in this case but we are unable to trace the potatoes after making enquiries'.

Interesting!

Inspector Poulton Catches Bill Gutteridge Drinking on Duty

George liked a regular pint, but as a policeman this simple pleasure was, of course, only generally allowed when he was off-duty. However, on one occasion at around 2.30pm in the afternoon in mid-February

1925 the temptation to have a quick pint was too much for Bill so as all was quiet he parked his bike against the wall of the 'Top Oak', (pictured), and went into the bar being met by Mrs Drane, the landlady.

The Royal Oak or 'Top Oak'as PC Bill Gutteridge would have known it. The old disused windmill can be seen to the far left of this photo.

Photo Courtesy of Stapleford Abbotts Historical Society

The old disused and derelict mill opposite the Royal Oak now demolished. Lady Decies' Beresford Tea Rooms and kennels were beside this.

Courtesy of Stapleford Abbotts Historical Society

He ordered and paid her a shilling for a pint of Whitbread bitter, also buying a beer for the only other person in the bar, a young man who was in the process of hanging a picture for Mrs Drane. George being George, who had accumulated a wealth of practical knowledge in his former employ in Norfolk offered, in between sips of beer, to help the young man with his task. But in the distance could be heard the sound of a motorcycle engine interrupting the quiet of the village, alerting George. The sound was familiar and became louder to the ear as it went up Oak Hill Road towards the Top Oak slowing to a halt right outside the pub. George recognised the individual sound of the bike much in the same way as he had heard the engine of the Morris Cowley belonging to Dr Lovell the morning he was killed.

There was then, a good chance this may be the motorcycle belonging to Inspector Poulton who patrolled the area. George asked Mrs Drane to put his beer, (or the remainder of it), behind the bar whilst he went outside to see who it was. George's intuition proved to be correct as he was confronted by Inspector Poulton who, on approaching the pub had noticed George's bike leaning up against the outside wall. The Inspector asked George what business he had in the pub. George replied saying 'I have just made a visit and helped a young man put up a picture in the bar for Mrs Drane' but the Inspector, with a doubtful expression on his face became increasingly suspicious of George's excuse for being in the pub at that time of the day stating sternly to George, 'Alright, I will make one as well'! Leaving George outside, Inspector Poulton entered the saloon bar doors at the front of the Oak which, incidentally have remained largely unchanged to this day, confronted Mrs Drane who, by now sensed trouble as the Inspector asked her directly what business PC Gutteridge had in the pub, at the same time cautioning her that if she did not tell the truth her licence could be at risk.

Understandably, this placed the now nervous Mrs Drane in an invidious position and in an attempt to 'pour oil on troubled waters' and to do her best to cover for George, she said that he had 'just come in for a biscuit' which unknown to Inspector Poulton was a term George used as a request for a pint of beer which on many previous visits was often placed discreetly and out of sight under his police helmet on a nearby shelf. But on this occasion the suspicious Inspector Poulton told Mrs Drane to retrieve George's remaining beer from under the counter on pain of compromising her licence if she lied. In the meantime George had been pacing up and down outside waiting for the Inspector to emerge and when he did, George tried to mitigate the situation by saying that he had been 'helping a young man put up a picture in the bar for Mrs Drane and thought he would have a pint while he was there'. Inspector Poulton said to George, 'I will have to report this' saying that 'you shouldn't have lied to me'. George argued that he was trying to help someone but Inspector Poulton pointed out that this was not police business so there was no reason to be in the pub. George then said in his broad and characteristic Norfolk dialect, 'It will go hard with me just shifting into this fresh house (2 Towneley Cottages) followed with a plea to the Inspector, 'Must you report it?' 'Yes' came the firm reply. The 'game was up' and there was no way out of this one for George.

He was fined a brutal 10 shillings, a hefty fine in 1925, for the combined offences of:

Drinking on Duty.

Entering Licensed Premises while on duty when his presence there was not required in the execution of duty.

(Quoted accurately from his Record of Service.)

This was unfortunate for George both financially and for his previously clean Record of Service which, prior to this incident had enjoyed a commendation in July 1923 from Captain Unett, the Chief Constable, for his perseverance and tact in arresting the three youths who had been trying to steal horses. George's record was now tarnished but the question remains; was he set up by a vengeful miscreant as it was known he certainly had adversaries as probably most policeman had (and always will), this being an expectation of the job, as criminals then and now will seek revenge on those who interrupt their criminal activities?

Evidence in the form of an extensive list of suspects following George's death were investigated on suspicion of being implicated with his murder. Could it have been one of those names, or a neighbour, some of whom who may have lived in the vicinity of which is evident in archived records, who did not 'see eye to eye' with the Gutteridges, who alerted Inspector Poulson to George's visits to the Oak, or was it an unfortunate - for George - coincidence? We will never know, of course, but my conversations with some long-standing members of the local community certainly consider that Bill had been watched and was 'set up' by those whose less than legitimate activities in the locality had been interrupted, or possibly as an act of revenge or deep resentment at the close presence of a policeman in their midst

Footnote: The Top Oak was a Whitbread House, and my grandfather's local where he drank all through the twenties and up until his death in 1956. He certainly would have known 'Bill' Gutteridge. John Lewin was a very loyal Drayman for the Whitbread Brewery in East London and would only drink Whitbread beer; often sending my mother Mabel to the 'Oak' with a jug to fetch him back some ale as other children often did. Archived records show that Bill Gutteridge would sternly question children he saw near the 'Oak' asking what they were doing there with the reply that they were fetching some beer for their parents. He then told them, 'Tell Mr Drane my helmet is on the shelf' – a pint of beer would then find its way beneath the police helmet as was the custom!

I can't help but wonder if my mother may have been one of those children?

CHAPTER 8

BILL GUTTERIDGE REPORTS AN ALLEGATION OF RAPE ON HIS BEAT

In his autobiography of 1956 entitled *Country Copper*, George 'Tot' Totterdell having retired with the rank of Detective Superintendent affectionately describes Bill Gutteridge as 'a typical country copper, stolid, loyal and not gifted with over-much imagination, a first-rate officer who controlled his "manor" with tact and zeal.'

But Bill Gutteridge obviously held his long time friend 'Tot' Totterdell in very high regard, seeking his advice on a very serious complaint which George obviously considered needed to be brought to the attention of those in higher authority. This occurred on one occasion when having travelled in person from Stapleford Abbotts late one Friday evening to Romford station in early 1926, Bill told Tot with much trepidation and seriousness in his voice that he had some important news to impart. Tot asked him what it was all about but Bill said 'I don't think I'd better say' and asking 'Is there anyone else on duty?' Implying that the news he had would require the attention of a high ranking officer.

Tot indicated that the Deputy Chief Constable Mr Howlett was in the building but offering a friendly caution to Bill said that 'Unless it's really important, I don't think I'd disturb him.' In great earnest, Bill replied, 'It's terribly important.' Seeing that his friend was deadly serious, Tot rang the Deputy Chief Constable's office whilst Bill sat looking very perturbed and concerned.

Tot showed Bill into the formidable Deputy Chief Constable's office announcing, 'PC Gutteridge to see you sir. He has something urgent to report.' After a considerable time, the Dep. Chief emerged and said to Detective Constable Totterdell, 'There has been a serious case of assault at Stapleford Abbotts, I want you to investigate it at once.'

Tot Totterdell reassured Bill saying 'I'll be over tomorrow morning' as Bill was leaving Romford Police Station late that evening for home. Bill, somewhat reassured said, 'I'm glad you're going to handle the case' and returned to Stapleford Abbotts.

In summary, the parents of a very pretty local Stapleford Abbotts girl whom Bill knew well had gone to Bill's home earlier that evening to report that their daughter, Elsie Torry had been raped having arrived home earlier almost naked, very distressed and covered in scratches. Elsie had told her parents that she had been walking along a nearby and deserted country lane and had been accosted by two men who had apparently dragged her into their car and taken her to a small wood some miles away, stripped off her clothes and assaulted her with the experience leaving her unconscious. Det. Constable Tot Totterdell had arrived the next morning (Saturday) to begin his investigation to find that there had been no further developments and that the girls clothes were still missing. Tot made enquiries in the locality, interviewing people in the vicinity and searching the scene of the alleged rape, a small area of foliage near some trees on a piece of wasteland. Det. Constable Totterdell noted that he found no evidence of such an assault i.e, no pieces of clothing or footprints in the earth that an assault of this nature involving three people had taken place with the soil and undergrowth remaining intact.

Tot went to the Torry family cottage in the village where Elsie lived with her parents and was shown into the sitting room. Tot says that Elsie entered the room almost immediately, (which it could be said seemed surprising for someone who had just endured such an assault!) and displaying some blushing of her face imparted her story to Tot (complete with all the attendant emotion) which was virtually the same as the account Bill Gutteridge gave to the Deputy Chief Constable. Tot pressed Elsie for more detail in which a vivid description of the two men, the Ford car involved, the terrible struggle to save her virtue, waking from unconsciousness to find herself almost naked, cut and bleeding.

Following Elsies story, Tot observed that, 'For a young and innocent girl who had suffered such an atrocious attack she appeared to me to have profited considerably from the nights' rest, further reflecting that, 'Her powers of recuperation, I felt, must have been quite out of the ordinary, as indeed must have been her will-power to banish so rapidly those moments of anguish which easily could in nightmarish memory could have persisted in haunting her for the remainder of her days'.

Sensing from Elsie's calm and collected delivery of her story that something was amiss, Tot put it to her that following extensive enquiries, he had 'found no evidence to support your story.' The game was up for Elsie whose indignant response cut no ice with Tot who then gave Elsie the opportunity to 'come clean' and the real truth was revealed. Elsie had met a young man with a car and they had gone to a quiet spot for an 'assignation' but afterwards regretted their actions and the possibility of a pregnancy which would have been difficult to explain to her parents and the social stigma which would follow in a close village community.

The young man left but Elsie panicked leaving her clothes under a bush at the roadside and deliberately walked through brambles to create physical evidence of an assault, arriving home in great distress to deliver to her shocked parents her concocted story complete with tears and scatches! Simply to cover her tracks should she have found herself to be pregnant. Tot said that, 'I later interviewed the girl's parents and persuaded them to look upon the affair charitably and with tolerance.

Nor, luckily, in the fullness of time were they forced to explain away the presence of a grandchild.'

Tot Totterdell took a statement from Elsie and before submitting it, showed it to Bill Gutteridge who was good friends with the Torry family who, in the words of Tot Totterdell said that Bill, in great disbelief was amazed and had known Elsie since childhood and that she had looked so innocent. Tot, in his book *Country Copper* said in reponse to Bill's surprise and disbelief that 'It isn't always advisable to trust our eyes'. A light-hearted comment he said he recalled and lamented in the aftermath of the tragically brutal murder of his friend the following year.

Records of the period show that after a period of service, police officers may apply for an additional increment of pay which would, if successful, Bill could expect to be paid 95 shillings a week as opposed to his current pay of 90 shillings per week. Bill made his application but also attended a promotion examination at Police Headquarters on the 10th January 1927 in his desire to make Sergeant which, if he was successful, would have increased his pay further to between 100 and 112 shillings and sixpence per week; a significant increase at the time. Unfortunately for Bill, he was unsuccessful on both counts. The results of his exam performance proved unsatisfactory and he failed; this being chanelled through to Superintendent Cant who then wrote to the Chief Constable advising him of the situation and as can be seen from the letter, Superintendent Cant did not hold Bill's performance as a policeman in particularly high regard. His original letter reads:

To the Chief Conatable of Essex (actual spelling from original letter)

P.C. 218 Gutteridge

I beg to report with reference to the above Constable that he is zealous in the discharge of his duties and no doubt does his duty to the best of his ability, I cannot say that he is intelligent of proficient, he attended the examination for promotion at Head Quarters on the 10th January 1927 and failed, his reports are very badly written, I would respectfully suggest that the additional increment be held over for twelve months to give him an opportunity to improve.

Michael Cant Superintendent

After consideration, the Chief Constable produced a memo for Bill Gutteridge in which he states that;

'It is not sufficient that a Constable should do his work conscientiously and to the best of his ability, he must in addition, be keen to show proof that he is making a real effort to improve himself in his knowledge of police matters.

It will be observed that under para. 60 Police Regulations, a Constable who has not been granted an additional increment of pay, can apply for reconsideration of his case when he has served a further period of twelve months.

Please hand this to P.C. 218 Gutteridge for retention by him,

Chief Constable.'

It can be appreciated that this correspondence would have been a great disappointment to Bill. Superintendent Cant's damning report to the Chief Constable is very unfortunate in that he seems to be unaware that Bill had had minimal elementary education, hence poorly written reports and having to support his mother from a very early age. Bill, of course, was noted for being zealous in his duties this being tragically illustrated in his brief encounter with Browne and Kennedy later that year in the early morning of 27th September 1927.

George Oversleeps and Misses a Conference Point

George had returned home at 10.30pm from an earlier duty for sleep and some rest, setting his alarm clock for 12.15am in readiness for his 12.30am night patrol. George awoke and with horror discovered it was ten minutes past two! He dressed in record time and went out on his beat, reaching the conference point at How Green outside and opposite Grove House at 2.45am instead of the required time of 2am. There were no other officers to meet George at Howe Green as PC Taylor was off duty on a rest day. George, respectfully and on his own initiative volunteered a very honest and apologetic letter to his superior Inspector Poulton dated the 22nd April 1927, outlining the reason for his late arrival to the conference; 'I found that the alarm clock had failed owing to me failing to release the switch when I had set it for 12.15am,' further stating that, 'This is the first point I have missed or been late at during the whole of my service'.

Inspector Poulton forwarded Bill's letter to Superintendent Michael Cant for his consideration and I would suggest that Bill's honesty had appealed to his superiors, who decided that no further action would be taken as this letter contained a logical explanation of human error coupled with a sincere apology. The actual letter opposite, by kind permission and courtesy of the Essex Police Museum.

It is worthy of note and probably to George's amusement that in previous times on the 23rd May 1913 his good friend, Tot Totterdell as a 'rookie' policeman had been reported for missing two conference points, one at Westcliff station at 1pm and the other at Westcliff Bridge at 1.30am having missed both of these as he had been in the porter's room at the railway station during these times. Despite giving a written explanation to his superiors this was not accepted by the Chief Constable Mr E. M. Showers who wrote on May 27th 1913; 'This young Constable is severely cautioned to attend his C.P.s properly, he had no business to shut himself up in the porter's room, where he could see nothing that was going on.'

Bill's letter

This severe warning so early in his police career probably brought Tot Totterdell down to earth and in later years this young and bright officer went on to become the first Detective Superintendent in the Essex County Constabulary but he was to face a double personal tragedy during the Second World War as both of his sons, serving with the Royal Navy during their military service (who also were both policemen), died when their ship was torpedoed and sunk by the enemy.

The Village 'Bobby' and the Poaching Community

Even some of Bill's old adversaries showed a special kind of respect they had for him including those within the poaching community. One most notable was a local poacher and formidable looking man, Walter Attridge, pictured below in later years, (the father of the very knowledgeable Margaret Sutton), was such a man who knew Bill Gutteridge well.

Walter Attridge

Photo by kind permission of Margaret and Tracy Sutton

Whilst on night patrol, Bill would occasionally catch Walter with his old shotgun, rabbit nets and an armful of rabbits and more often than not, Bill would issue Walter with a warning telling him to 'get off home', or 'I haven't seen you but leave a couple of rabbits on my gatepost and we'll say no more', earning Bill the nickname of 'Rabbit Come Nightly' in the community. However, on one occasion as Margaret Sutton informs me, Bill charged her father Walter with carrying a closed shotgun in a public place which, of course, could have been immediately discharged accidentally or otherwise and therefore a danger to the public. Walter attended court and was fined but this did not ruin their friendship as Walter realised that he had overstepped the mark and Bill had to do his job. But Bill had to tread a 'thin line' when dealing with farmers and poachers alike, advising one farmer in particular, Frank Aylett who had complained to Bill that 'there's somebody caning my rabbits something shocking,' further saying, 'I've got a feeling I know who it is'. Bill replied saying, 'I wouldn't say unless you're really sure' and to reassure Frank Aylett, said 'Don't worry, we'll ketch 'em'. Bill was reluctant in charging locals rather than outsiders he caught poaching, as he was fully aware of their circumstances in trying to make ends meet in those very austere times where the rabbit became an inexpensive part of their staple diet. In turning 'a blind eye' to some of their poaching activities the streetwise members of the community realised that Bill supported them in this way but on the other side of the coin Bill knew that if he came down hard on them, they could certainly have implicated him as a known and active poacher, often seen teaming up with the postman Harry Alexander on poaching expeditions at night when he was off duty.

Their 'nod' to Bill was by discreetly hanging a rabbit on his gatepost to have for dinner, could be interpreted as just their way of demonstrating their acceptance of him in their midst? It is unclear whether the other policemen in the vicinity i.e PCs Cameron and Taylor received the same 'community appreciation'? They may have done, although research does not imply this. Poaching has always been common in agricultural communities with examples of farmers and landowners adopting a 'flexible' attitude to this providing the local poachers do not become greedy and spoil it for everyone else. Despite that, in the 1920s the rabbit population had reached between 50 and 100 million in England with densities of 15 or 20 to the acre (50 to the hectare). With the introduction of myxomatosis in 1942 which decimated the rabbit population, a much favoured source of cheap food in rural communities had now taken a steep decline.

The reader could be forgiven for adopting a jaundiced view about Bill's dedication to policing and his 'questional behaviour' from time to time but in comparison with some of his close colleagues these are mild as I wish to explain. PC 'A', (although commended as was Bill Gutteridge), was disciplined for making false entries in his pocket book whilst another, PC 'B' was moved to another station due to inciting others to refuse orders as he had done so on several occasions himself and was considered to be 'difficult' to manage by senior police officers.

Hardly comparable with stopping for a pint when on duty which, I have been reliably informed from long serving retired officers and previously from my late uncle, PC Harold Lilley who was a policeman in Romford for many years, many policemen did drink on duty partly to keep their fingers on the 'pulse of the community' which they policed in those times but this remained, of course, 'unofficial' never being referred to and assumed by many as part of a policeman's work.

CHAPTER 9

MONDAY THE 26TH SEPTEMBER 1927 AND BILL'S LAST CASE

That day, the 26th September 1927, Bill had gone to see Mr Alexander Veryard at his farm to let him know that he had found some iron gates that Veryard had reported stolen and would need him to make a statement but as they proceeded to the house they were met by Mr Stevens, a local haulage contractor, who kept a Fordson tractor on Veryard's farm saying it had been tampered with and could not be moved. Mr Stevens suspected that Mr Veryard had been the culprit and virtually accused him of damaging the machine. True to his character, Veryard told him to get off his property. At this point Veryard and Bill went into the house for Veryard to make the statement about the alleged 'stolen' gates with Veryard asking Bill if he would talk again to Mr Stevens about the tractor. In the meantime, Mr Stevens had not left the farm and waited outside.

Bill took the statement from Mr Veryard and they went outside to find Mr Stevens still there who further accused Mr Veryard of damaging his tractor and again, was told to get off the property. Bill and Mr Stevens left the farm and both had a light lunch at Bill's police cottage with Rose in attendance where they talked at length about the disabled tractor and his complaint against Mr Veryard. Later in the afternoon after Bill had completed his reports and other paperwork, Mr Veryard arrived to sign his statement and to provide Bill with a list of other items which he said had been stolen but his well-known eccentric behavour spontaneously surfaced to the surprise of Rose and, possibly less surprisingly to George, when after being offered a cup of tea by Rose of which he drank half, in the words of Rose, he 'got up and took my husband's helmet off a nail and tried to put the helmet on his head. He said, "This reminds me of a big mansion where I used to be where they had a truncheon". My husband at once took it away from him and asked him to sign the statement.'

It had been rumoured that Alexander Veryard had spent some time in a mental institution and the sight of Bill's truncheon had given him a 'flashback' to those times in a big institution, the proportions and image of which could resemble a mansion as did the large lunatic asylum at Warley? Veryard did not leave immediately and dragged his heels signing the statement despite Rose giving him the usual social prompts that it was time to leave such as opening the back door for him but even this caused him to be difficult further by announcing 'No, I'll go out the front way.' Rose, as a policeman's wife was expected to be of assistance to her husband in a lesser role being to some extent the ears and eyes of her neighbourhood but to be a 'listening ear' in the guise of an unpaid social worker, listener, confidant and counsellor and it is extremely likely that George and Rose had many 'interesting' confidential conversations about the people and events in their community.

Early that same evening, Bill cycled in the direction of Passingford Bridge, meeting and talking with a local labourer called Mr Glasscock and hence, possibly up to where Mr Veryard lived at the grand and picturesque Albyns Farmhouse (later to occupied by the aristocratic Loyd family) near Stapleford Tawney to look at the damaged tractor but returned by 9pm for supper with Rose.

Bill obviously took into account the erratic behaviours of this old farmer that he had got to know, as he had with most of the others in the village and that Veryard was unpredictable and eccentric. His threats to shoot Bill were regarded by this wise village policeman as regular and hollow threats as on one occasion when he was overheard threatening to shoot Bill, who remarked blithely to the listener, 'Oh! He's threatened to shoot me on many occasions'. Although at the time Bill knew this was very unlikely to happen and took it 'with a pinch of salt'. This overheard threat quickly reached the detectives in charge of the subsequent murder investigation so it transpired that Veryard was understandably one of the first to be interviewed following the murder and high on the very extensive list of suspects.

Rose and her children must have been safely asleep in their beds as Bill was returning home with his old cycle from his night patrol having dutifully stayed at his conference point opposite the gates at Grove House at How Green until 3.25am, discussing with PC Sydney Taylor their police work of the day. The conversation featured the previously described ongoing problems Bill had been having with the eccentric, argumentative, and difficult local farmer Mr Veryard and the complaint of damage to the Fordson tractor levelled at him by local haulage contractor Mr Stevens, not helped by the bad feelings that existed between them. Their conference drew to a close with PC Taylor having left a little earlier to go home down Hook Lane to his Police Cottage at Lambourne End for his cocoa and then to bed. Bill checked his watch and made his way downhill towards Pinchback Bridge passing Rose Cottage, quietly enshrouded in the early morning mist and on in the direction of his cottage in Tysea Hill where he intended to complete his paperwork before retiring to bed and tragically, as history records, Bill never finished his shift or arrived home alive.

PC Sydney Taylor had arrived at his Lambourne End police cottage at around 4.30am apparently not having heard the sound of four loud Webley Service Revolver gunshots which had taken the life of his colleague Bill Gutteridge a short time after what was to be their last meeting at How Green Hill, brutally shattering the early morning peace of Stapleford Abbotts.

CHAPTER 10

THE NIGHTMARE BEGINS

Busily engaged in getting Bill's breakfast ready, getting Muriel ready for school and little Jack dressed, the normal morning chores and listening to the sounds of the day Rose was now busily hanging out her washing on this bright Tuesday morning in late September unaware of the gathering crowd of policemen, press and local people outside the front of her home, Rose was surprised to see the ashen-faced Rev. James William Armitage arrive who, on learning the dreadful news of Bill's murder had immediately left his home at the Old Rectory (pictured) close to St. Mary the Virgin, the Parish Church of Stapleford Abbotts.

After being allowed through the police barriers blocking the section of the road where the body of George lay some distance away, the Reverend Armitage, arriving with some apprehension and having passed the scene of the murder turned into Tysea Hill to be faced with what appeared to be an urgently growing 'circus' of reporters, cameramen, policemen and onlookers in this small community.

Making his way through the front gate of the guarded county police house, his unenviable role was to be the courier of the worst shock poor Rose was ever to experience; that her loving husband and the well respected village policeman Bill Gutteridge had been found brutally murdered and lay lifeless a short distance from the cottage where they lived in Tysea Hill.

Rose, whose mind was already swirling and questioning the attention and commotion her cottage was suddenly exposed to and thinking it very unusual and strange that neighbours were entering

The Old Rectory, home of the Rev. Armitage.

Courtesy of the Stapleford Abbotts Historical Society

St. Mary the Virgin, Parish Church of Stapleford Abbotts.

Courtesy of Stapleford Abbotts Historical Society

her house without a word, unaware at this point that George was dead, went into a state of collapse on being told the news by the Rev. Armitage, Rose seemingly being the last to know as the late Muriel Alexander explained.

The neighbours, supportively waiting around including the incredibly strong and humanitarian Gertrude, Lady Decies (pictured below).

Courtesy of Tatler Magzine and Wikipedia.com

Lady Decies, decorated in WW1 as a war hero having been mentioned in 'Dispatches', and as a civilian a prominent dog and cat fancier, ran her own Beresford Tea Gardens and dog 'hotel' living in a house close to the old windmill opposite the Royal Oak pub. She had reported to the initial police enquiry that she had heard revolver gunshots and a car roar by in the early hours, as did several others in the local vicinity, including Mr 'Monty' Montague Martin at Mitchell's Farm close to How Green, later saying that he thought it may be the sound of poachers shooting nearby. Lady Decies of course recognised, and had been able to differentiate the sound of these as revolver shots instead of rifle fire as these would have been very familiar to her having bravely served for a large part of the Great War at the Western front and in Russia during the Bolshevic revolution as a nurse in the battle-clearing stations, despite the pain of losing her very young son early in her marriage and then tragically in 1910, the sudden death of her husband.

She had also been wounded by shellfire describing her injuries as a 'mere scratch on the arm'. Vivid descriptions of her experiences as a nurse dealing with the huge numbers of the dead and wounded arriving at the clearing stations were very graphic and detailed and not for the squeamish. Rose would now, at her time of unexpected and brutal loss have had beside her probably the best placed, most experienced and unshockable ally in 'Molly' (as she was known by the wounded soldiers in her care, her first name being Maria), together with Rose's sister Agnes and her husband Frank Cross, gathering family members and close friends in her time of raw and profound grief.

Lady Decies had already been made aware of the terrible tragedy that had unfolded, kindly offering Rose immediate support as the news was broken, comforting her as she sat sobbing and inconsolable at the kitchen table probably considering this to all be a bad dream; her mind swirling with mixed emotions and disbelief. Rose was lucky to be surrounded by a host of genuinely supportive and protective neighbours at this terrible time in the close community of Stapleford Abbotts some of whom and probably including Lady Decies in the not too distant past, had probably played a familiar and unenviable role in comforting other mothers and their children, daughters and girls, betrothed to soldiers whose hearts sank and their worlds collapsed on receiving that dreaded brown telegram from the war office announcing in a short almost impersonal message, that that their loved ones were 'missing, presumed dead' or having been 'killed in action', never to return from 'the war to end all wars'.

They were sympathetic and empathic to some extent in the pain and sense of loss poor Rose must have been feeling but as events will portray, this was just the beginning.

Muriel Gutteridge had left home on Tuesday morning the 27th September and gone to the council elementary school at Havering-Atte-Bower (pictured below) some distance away in Havering at the normal time, unaware of the terrible events which were to change her and her family's life forever earlier that morning.

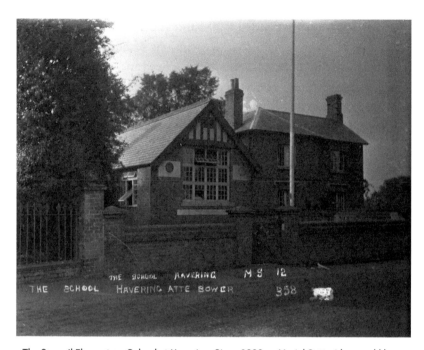

The Council Elementary School at Havering, Circa. 1930 as Muriel Gutteridge would have known it.

By kind permission of Havering Library Local studies

Now the lovely Dame Tipping School.

Picture by author

Shortly after arriving she was called to the school office where she was met by the head teacher Mr Derrick who enquired of Muriel 'Is everything alright at home?' with Muriel replying, 'Yes Sir'. 'Are you sure?' enquired Mr Derrick. 'Yes sir' reiterated Muriel but Mr Derrick, by now most likely aware of Bill's death through the village grapevine and the growing commotion, said 'You had better go home and see' and Muriel went home immediately. She ran all the way back alone from Havering to Towneley Cottages, a distance of nearly a mile although her neighbour and fellow pupil John Alexander the son of the postman Harry Alexander, offered to go with her but he was not allowed to. These were early signs that John genuinely cared and felt protective towards his young neighbour and friend Muriel who had smiled at each other over the garden fence, immediately becoming sweethearts. In later years hence they would become man and wife with the blessing of Rose.

A plethora of thoughts and questions were running through Muriel's young mind as she vividly describes many years later in a recorded interview with retired Essex Police Inspector Dr Maureen Scollan. As it was washing day had the 'copper' (a wood and coal-fired boiler used by most people in those times to clean clothes) in the corner of the scullery boiled over and burnt her mother? Breathless, young Muriel arrived at her home at 2, Towneley Cottages, to be faced with a 'hubbub' of press, policemen and onlookers. The village seemed to have come to a halt with an animated crowd having gathered in Tysea Hill outside the county police house as Muriel was ushered through the clamouring crowd into her home by a policeman. Muriel was surprised and confused to see her distraught mother sitting at the table being comforted by close friends and neighbours; Muriel's world collapsing on being told that her father had been shot by someone early that morning and was dead. Muriel now had to face the reality that, at 12 years old her loving and so proud father was never to return. This whole surreal scenario must have seemed like a bad dream to Muriel and it was only the support of her grieving mother, Aunt Agnes (known as 'Peg'), and her husband Frank Cross and later their daughter, Muriel's cousin Olive and close neighbours who together provided some comfort to Muriel and her little brother Alfred 'Little Jackie' as Muriel called him. (pictured).

An exceptionally touching and spontaneous picture of Muriel and her little brother, Alfred (Jack) taken in happier times.

Courtesy of Mr Brian Alexander

Muriel and Jack had last seen their father early on Monday of the 26th September, the evening before, when they were put to bed, feeling safe that their 'Daddie' as he liked to be known, was preparing to go on night duty and quite possibly were asleep by this time never hearing the front door click shut at around 11pm as their father, resplendent in his blue/black serge uniform and helmet, donned his heavy cape and left his cottage displaying the blue plaque of the County Police (pictured), and rode off on his trusty old police cycle into the cold, dark and misty September night for the last time.

Courtesy of the Essex Police Museum, Chelmsford.

Picture by author

The Mailbag Delivery Driver Alec Ward Makes an Horrific Discovery

Bill Gutteridge had lain in the roadway for approximately 3 hours before being discovered at around 6.30 in the morning by William Alec Ward, delivering sacks of mail to the post offices on his round; the last one being at the post office near to where the postman Harry Alexander, another wounded war hero of WW1 lived at 3, Towneley Cottages in Tysea Hill.

William Aleck Ward, standing by his Ford Model T Tourer.
By kind permission of Pamela Ward and the Ward Family

On that still and very misty September morning dawn was breaking as Alec drove carefully northwards toward Ongar and on to his next mail bag drop-off point at Stapleford Tawney Post Office in his Model T Ford Tourer. Approaching a slight bend on the incline of this narrow country road, Alec saw in the beams of his headlamps a partially huddled figure with legs stretched out into the road. Initially thinking it may have been a tramp or vagrant, he stopped his vehicle and nervously getting out approached the huddled figure, realising as he got closer that it was a policeman. Alec, seeing the helmet laying near to the figure, shouted out 'Is that you Bill?' and as he drew closer in the heavy mist, he was filled with horror to discover that this was indeed, his long-time friend and the village policeman he had seen many times in the village and on his early morning round, PC Bill Gutteridge.

The Old Romford looking north to Ongar road showing the spot (offcentre right) where Alec Ward discovered the body of Bill Gutteridge.

Courtesy of the Essex Police Museum

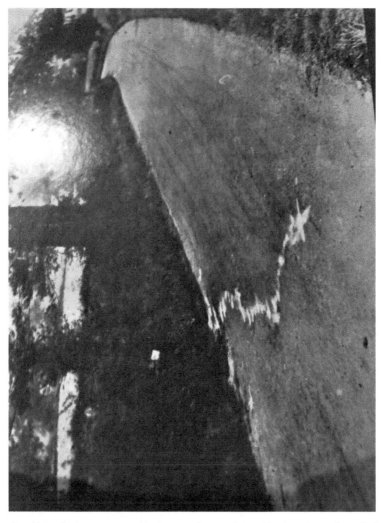

The Old Romford to Ongar Road looking south towards Pinchback Bridge and Romford showing the actual spot Bill Gutteridge was murdered. Carbolic powder was sprinkled on the blood trails to highlight the scene of the killing as evidence. Notice the sign on the tree marking the spot which remained there long after the event and the tyre marks made partly by the Morris Cowley as the killers sped away from the scene and probably by the Model T Ford driven by Alec Ward as he drove away fast to Stapleford Tawney to alert the authorities.

Courtesy of the EssexPoliceMuseum

The B175 Romford to Ongar road as it is today with tall sparsely-leaved tree centre of picture marking the approximate place parallel to the old road where Alec Ward discovered the body of PC Bill Gutteridge, 638 yards south of Grove House. Gutteridge lane can be seen towards the top of the picture on the right and curves round to Rose Cottage to meet the Roadside Memorial to Bill Gutteridge. (See Retracing Bill's last walk with his first grandson Brian Alexander.)

Photo by author

Alec again shouted through the swirl of the heavy mist 'What's the matter Bill?' now fearing that he too, may possibly be attacked by the same assailant he thought may be hiding in the bushes ready to attack again and that his valuable sacks of post for which he was responsible, would be stolen along with his mail vehicle. Now, in the still and very misty dark of the early morning, Alec leant over the body to find Bill Gutteridge's hands cold and lifeless; a light frost having formed on the torn and heavy police cape Bill wore. Meanwhile, Mr Richard Warren, a local bus driver living at nearby High House Farm had stopped his motorbike as he rode from his driveway to see what had happened thinking quite logically at first that Bill Gutteridge had been a victim of a hit and run driver or as others had speculated, that he had been hit over the head by an assailant.

Alec quickly told him that this was not the case and that it appeared to him that Bill Gutteridge had been shot, as suspected by PC John Bloxham from nearby Havering-Atte-Bower, one the the first officers on the scene and confirmed later by Dr Robert Woodhouse who had been called out to attend the body. However, Dr Woodhouse indicated to the inquest later that week that the bullet wounds were hidden by the amount of blood on the victim's face.

By now, others going about their early morning business had begun to gather to see what had happened to their village 'Bobby' including Titch Dolman who also stopped whilst on his way to Lord Lambourne's estate. Titch was also told that Bill Gutteridge was dead but shocked to be told this, Titch had to go on his way as he had to collect some peas for a big dinner at one of the big houses locally.

An early winter image of Rose Cottage courtesy of the owners, Mr and Mrs Rogers (date unknown) in a sadly dilapidated state but with hidden beauty nonetheless!

A recent image of the beautiful 14th century Rose cottage,
courtesy of the owners Mr and Mrs Rogers.

Picture by author

Alec instructed Richard Warren to keep watch over the body while he ran for help. Alec, a young man, sprinted the 250 yards up the road to Rose Cottage where his shouting and vigorous knocking on the door awoke the occupier Mr Alfred Perritt a local insurance agent, with Alec, breathlessly and excitedly explaining to him of his dreadful discovery as they walked quickly down the road to where PC Gutteridge lay.

(Approximate distance quoted by Alfred Perritt under cross-examination by Mr Roome, documented in *The Trial of Browne and Kennedy*). It reads:

'Alfred Peritt, examined by Mr Roome - "I am an insurance agent, and I live at Rose Cottage, How Green. On the morning of the

27th September last, about six 'o clock, I was wakened by Mr Ward knocking at the door. I at once dressed, and, in consequence of what he told me, I went out with him in the direction of Romford about 250 yards from my house. It is downhill. As we went along, I saw the body of PC Gutteridge"…'

As Richard Warren was keeping watch over the body on the look-out for approaching vehicles, by this time, the sun was starting to shine and very slowly burning away the mist, and a growing band of local people including farmer John Sayward from Stapleford Hall, farmer Montague Martin from nearby Mitchell's Farm and others going about their early morning business, stood in shock at what they saw.

The village sign at Stapleford Tawney with the beautiful Old Post Office in the background.
Picture by author

Alec urgently needed to access a telephone for help, as at the time private telephones were for the privileged few but there existed a very informal arrangement beween senior officers and those wealthy enough to have telephones and landowners such as Lord Lambourne who made their telephones available to senior police officers in times of crisis or emergencies.

In the meantime, Alfred Perritt, having initially tried vainly to revive Bill with smelling salts was told by a passing local roadworker Mr George Murrell that Bill was already dead, decided to lift George's outstretched legs in towards the verge of the narrow lane and parallel to the bank where he had fallen to prevent them being run over by other vehicles which may have been travelling north towards Ongar and had not seen the dark shape of Bill's body lying in the slight uphill gradient of the half-light of this still misty country road. (This action had to be explained to senior officers most notably Detective Inspector John Crockford who had arrived first to start the investigation, and at the trial of Browne and Kennedy) as it interfered with a scene of a murder.

In 1927 the old B175 at How Green in Stapleford Abbotts was only a narrow country lane, only 17 feet 6 inches wide where Bill Gutteridge was killed.

Part of the old Romford to Ongar road (B175) looking south towards Pinchback Bridge from Rose Cottage as it is today and largely unchanged having escaped the main road reprofiling of later years.

Picture by author

Part of the old Romford to Ongar road (B175) looking North on the approach to Rose Cottage, a familiar sight to 'Bill' Gutteridge on his Police bicycle and to Alec Ward driving his Ford Model T tourer.

The road at the top right of the picture leads down to Mitchells Farm

Picture by author

Due to his prompt action in raising the alarm and taking a furious drive to Stapleford Tawney Post Office in a desperate attempt to alert the authorities, the role of Alec in this terrible event is much understated. From here he telephoned Romford Police Station but surprisingly and very frustratingly for Alec, the operator would not put the emergency call through as PC Gutteridge was not actually stationed there, although he was a member of the Essex Constabulary! Even in those days, rules were exceptionally rigid.

The indignant and determined Alec was advised by the Romford Police operator to telephone the Police station at Ongar. With growing frustration, he immediately telephoned the switchboard and asked to be put through to Ongar Police explaining to the operator of his grim discovery and that this was a very serious incident. Alec, still in a state of anxiousness, was told the call would not be put through unless he paid the call fee of five old pence (two new pence). Without any money on him, this ridiculous situation incensed Alec and an argument with the operator ensued which was rising in intensity until the Stapleford Tawney postmistress Mrs Knight intervened and using her level of authority, instructed the operator to process the call forthwith with the now still 'bristling' with frustration, Alec Ward, being given the chance to explain his terrible discovery.

Alec returned to where Bill lay to provide the now growing group of locals awaiting news and information about his attempts to alert the authorities and what would happen next. The investigation and massive manhunt was signalled by the arrival of senior Essex County Constabulary detectives and indeed the Chief Constable, Captain John Alfred Unett attended the scene to assess the situation for himself and by 12.15pm that same day he had sent a request to Scotland Yard for one of their CID detectives to take charge of the enquiry such was the gravity of this terrible crime and it read:

The dead body of a PC was found at about 6a.m. 27th *September near*

Romford. Everything points to a brutal murder. The C.C. desires the assistance of a Scotland [Yard] C.I.D. officer and will be glad if this can be arranged. The officer deputed should communicate with Detective Insp. Crockford at Romford 79.

Detective Inspector John Crockford, formerly a farm labourer from Southwold in Suffolk and the first senior officer to attend the murder scene

Detective Chief Inspector James Berrett was the only real and popular choice for this assignment and having just solved his most recent murder case involving the shooting of a Brixton cab driver, Berrett and Detective Sergeant John Harris immediately left for Romford first arriving in mid-afternoon and then much later, Stapleford Abbotts. The investigation was now under way with a vengeance but this unnecessary delay allowed much more time for the (then unknown) killers, Frederick Guy Browne and William Henry Kennedy, to be many miles away with Dr Lovell's bloodstained and damaged Morris Cowley being discovered abandoned later that morning in a Brixton alleyway.

The inquest into the murder was opened on Friday 30th September 1927 at the Romford Institution by the coroner Mr C. Edgar Lewis, the jury consisting of Capt. A.J. Dyer (foreman), Mr F.W. Jones, Mr G.J.P. Arnold, Mr F. Hobday,Mr G. Darby, Mr W. R. Ley, Mr W. Brunsden, Mr H. Poston and Mr A.R. Tuff. Also in attendance was Chief Inspector James Berrett, Detective Inspector Crockford and Inspector Denny of Romford Police who was in charge of the inquest arrangements.

Before the inquest proceeded, Mr Lewis, on behalf of the court addressed those assembled offering sympathy and condolences to Rose, her children, the family, extending these to the Chief Constable and his officers for the loss they had all suffered resulting from the brave actions of PC George Gutteridge. Faced with this daunting assembly of formidable officers and members of the judiciary, the first to enter was George's mother Mrs Mary Edwards, followed by Agnes Cross and the pitifully distraught and near to collapse, Rose Gutteridge, accompanied by PC Sydney Taylor.

The unceasing pain and grief poor Rose was enduring was compounded by being the first to be called to give evidence at which she burst into tears and in a quiet trembling voice, confirmed her full name and address. Rose told the inquest that she had attended the mortuary to identify her husband's body, collapsing as she continued to give evidence but was given smelling salts and assisted by those around her to regain her composure. During the latter stages of the inquest, Capt. Dyer the foreman of the jury said that the jury would like to know the cause of the delay in sending for the doctor? Detective Inspector John Crockford said that he only received news of the death of PC Gutteridge at 7.45am on the morning of the murder, arriving at Stapleford Abbotts at approximately 8am before sending for the doctor whose practice was in South Street Romford, using the taxi he had employed.

The Coroner, in further questioning the delay pointed out that an hour had elapsed between Det. Inspector Crockford receiving the news and Dr Woodhouse being called. (DI Crockford had been examining the body and the scene of the murder during this time.)

Mr Lewis, in adjourning the court until the 26th November 1927 (date as quoted from death certificate), said he would consider the evidence and allow significant time for the police enquiry to proceed.

At the adjourned inquest into the death of PC Gutteridge, on the 25th November 1927 in Romford, the telephone operator, Harold Thomas Murdoch who argued with Alec Ward about the call fee demanding that Alec should pay the charge of five pence before the call would be put through, was called to account. His supervisor Mr Edwin Henry Carter and Mr William Benham, Superintendent of Traffic on the London Telephone System were also called by the Coroner Mr C. Edgar Lewis Esq to account for their actions and to give evidence as a result of statements made by Alec Ward soon after the murder.

It was found that the operator Harold Thomas Murdoch was acting under instructions from Edwin Carter his supervisor but despite this, he conceded that the call 'should have gone through without question' but Traffic Superintendent William Benham stated to the Coroner that he had instructed all telephone staff 'to pass on all police calls without question'. It is subject to speculation whether this instruction was made before the murder, but more than likely following the event (as will be seen later). It suggests from the court report that 'ironically' there were inconsistencies in operational protocols and 'communication' between senior and operational staff in the London Telephone System?

A major point raised during the inquest into the death of PC Gutteridge was that of police in outlying and rural areas having very little access to a telephone and the jury after returning their verdict of wilful murder. But before retiring, the jury added a rider stating; 'That they considered that special telephone facilities should be given to the police, and that every policeman in outlying districts should have a telephone at his house'. Detective Inspector Crockford transmitted this recommendation by the jury to Superintendent Attridge who then forwarded it directly to the Chief Constable for his information who was quoted later in the The *Essex Weekly News* as saying that; 'although telephones had been installed in many police stations and police houses, all the telephones in the world wouldn't have prevented PC Gutteridge from being murdered'. However, in the circumstances, some things are better left unsaid.

True perhaps, but arguably the killers may have been apprehended sooner if more telephones had been made available and the delay in contacting Dr Woodhouse to attend the murder scene to assess the body of Bill Gutteridge had not occurred is unclear. The *Essex Weekly News* was very quick to launch its own campaign for better telephone communications in rural areas which was endorsed by the National Federation of Women's Institutes and gained huge public support, further encouraging the AA and RAC Motoring organisations to provide keys to the police for their own call boxes which at the time were being installed on trunk roads. Soon after the recommendations made by the inquest, the authorities acted quickly with a public notice being posted in the *Daily Mail* on the 8th May 1928 informing that signs were being attached to all telephone boxes in London and announcing to the public that emergency calls to the Police, Fire Brigade and Ambulance Service would be immediately put through with all operators being given strict instructions to do this without delay. It also went on to state that if an automatic call box was used, the two pence required to use this will be refunded after the call has been made and that eventually these notices would be attached to telephone boxes throughout the country.

The 999 emergency call system was now in its infancy and by June 1937 following the death of five women in a serious fire at the residence of a surgeon in Wimpole Street London, at the height of which a close neighbour had frustratingly been kept in a long queue by the Welbeck Telephone Exchange. Incensed, he wrote to the *Times* newspaper about his fruitless attempts to contact the fire brigade in such dire and tragic circumstances, resulting in multiple deaths. A government enquiry ensued and resulting from this, the 999 emergency call system had now been born.

The urgency of Alec Ward's supreme efforts immediately following the tragic murder of his friend PC Gutteridge had identified a real 'black hole' in how telephone communications were inadequate in emergency situations especially in outlying districts and villages, so the passionate actions of Alec Ward deserve commendation for his tenacious part in alerting through his own difficulty, the authorities of this shortfall and urgent need for change.

The enormous impact this brutal and needless murder of a much respected and dedicated village policeman, the only murder of a policeman in this village to date cannot be understated, shaking Stapleford Abbotts and the outraged nation to the core; shining the national and international spotlight on this otherwise quiet and rural Essex community. The fact that a report of the murder was even featured in a Chicago newspaper further illustrated the magnitude in a global sense, the 'ripple' effect of public shock and indignation that this kind of brutality should visit a sleepy rural English village where it was so alien, and yet sadly familiar in the mean streets of 1920's Chicago where territorial and prohibition-fuelled gangland violence erupted regularly.

This type of crime was thankfully, a very rare occurrence in rural Essex, not having re-occurred to date and only similar to that of the brutal murder of Sergeant Eves in 1893 at Purleigh near Maldon, which resulted in countrywide abhorrence and shock. This also caused widespread shock to the community and beyond, due to the brutality of the act which further demonstrates the challenges, often violent, that policemen had to face, armed only with a truncheon, a whistle and an electric torch to find their way in dark country lanes and even on main roads before electric street lighting, with no recourse to radio communication and with very little access to telephones.

A Village is left in Shock and disbelief

The press and onlookers, some genuine in their concern, melted away. Rose, consumed by grief and needing help to stand, demonstrated an innate selflessness and strength that only dedicated mothers display by instinctively protecting and comforting their children; her daughter Muriel now at 12 years old and little four-year-old Jack whose birthday on the 19th September was just over a week before, would have looked around amid the confusion and drama with his young mind trying to make sense of it all probably and mercifully, not being able to understand what all the fuss and excitement was about as very young children do in these circumstances.

The quiet rural Essex village of Stapleford Abbotts was now under the spotlight of public attention having suddenly been cast onto the world stage; 'swarming with policemen' as a local farmer, now in his nineties recollected to me. Little Muriel did not, as expected, see her father alive again as he lay in the coach house at the Top Oak awaiting post mortem the next day. I would hazard a guess that she was encouraged by Rose, friends and neighbours to remember him as she saw him last.

Without George, who now lay, face covered, cold and still in the coach house at the rear of the Royal Oak with a policeman standing guard over the lifeless body of his colleague, Rose must have experienced an almost surreal, huge void and emptiness that had brutally entered her life as she sat dazed and tearful in the cottage she had shared with her husband George, who kissed her late the previous evening for the last time and to unknowingly embark upon his last shift as one of the village and community policemen; always being the 'rock' in Rose and her young family's life.

A Final Salute to Bill From the Poaching Community

The loss of Bill Gutteridge hit Walter Attridge, a prominent and well known local poacher and friend of Bill Gutteridge hard, with

An early and classic photograph of George and his little daughter Muriel.

Courtesy of Mr Brian Alexander

Margaret Sutton (his daughter) telling me that during the Tuesday morning whilst the village was still teeming with police, her father left the noisy crowds and went up to the 'Top Oak' (pictured) to 'say his goodbyes' and pay his respects to his friend and sometime adversary, Bill who lay very still in the guarded coach house.

The Royal Oak in the 1920s with the coach house on the right where Bill's body was taken through the double doors (to the left of the building) and laid out on a trestle after his murder. A police guard stood watch over the body before it was taken to Oldchurch Hospital by ambulance the next day for a post-mortem examination by Dr Robert Woodhouse.

Courtesy of the Stapleford Abbotts Historical society

The Royal Oak recently renamed as the 'Top Oak' as it is in modern times with the frontage remaining largely unchanged.

Picture by author

Sadly, Walter was not allowed through the part-open doors by the policeman guarding the body from unauthorised access, most notably the invasive press, and from any 'ghouls' which may have tried to view the body as this was still regarded as part of a crime scene and still had to be protected for forensic examination and investigation.

But recognising and realising that Walter was genuine in his sorrow wishing to bid his last goodbye to his compatriot, the astute police guard allowed Walter to stand just outside the open doors and look into the coach house where he could clearly see his friend Bill Gutteridge lying on a trestle with pennies covering his empty eyes, a common practice used in those times to keep the eyelids of the deceased closed but for Bill Gutteridge this was somehow symbolic in maintaining the dignity of this brave man in death. Other countries have observed the same practice over the centuries but signifying different cultural meanings in preparation for the next life.

'I'll miss you mate' were the last words Walter spoke to his friend as he turned for home.

The very sad Walter returned home and we can't help but wonder if his desire for poaching was ever quite the same again. Word of Bill's murder reached the Bishop of Barking, Dr James Inskip who, from this moment on would be a pillar of strength to Rose and her children. He left his duties with some urgency that same evening to travel over to Stapleford Abbotts to visit Rose and to offer her comfort and support.

The intrusive press 'jackals' seemingly indifferent to her grief, still pestered Rose, offering her money for her life story which, in her dignity Rose firmly rejected, seeing this to be an immoral offer considering that she would be profiteering from the death of her husband if she had accepted. If she had it would have exposed her to further comments and condemnation from the same village gossips who tried to smear her character previously in addition to compromising her strong sense of morality.

CHAPTER 11

ROSE FACES A FORMIDABLE NEW CHALLENGE

The village of Stapleford Abbotts, still in shock and with a host of strangers asking continual questions, would rally in support, including Mr Harry Alexander the postman and his wife Ethel who lived at No.3 Towneley Cottages with their family, offering Rose and her children a bedroom for that Tuesday night as a frightened Rose could not bear to stay in her own cottage at No.2, now a desolate and unhappy place. From this point on, the Alexander and Cross families became the saviours of Rose, Muriel and Jack in the terrible aftermath of the death of Bill Gutteridge. A cloud of sadness and disbelief had descended over the village as it was coming to terms with this senseless and brutal murder of 'one of their own' and *their* village policeman as George had become. Bill's body was removed from the coach house at the Royal Oak the next day (Wednesday) and taken by ambulance to the mortuary at Oldchurch Hospital Romford, to undergo a post-mortem examination by physician Dr Robert Woodhouse and the search for further forensic evidence and clues into the circumstances of his death which may help to identify his killer or killers.

In the days following, the still devastated and now widowed Rose Gutteridge, being the next of kin and very likely being accompanied and supported by her sister Agnes and her husband Frank Cross, had to attend the mortuary to identify the body of her husband Bill which lay in a bleak, white tiled cold room at the former Oldchurch Hospital and covered by a mortuary shroud. This nightmarish situation is something no one, especially a young woman such as Rose, should have to perform in any circumstance, being presented with the sadly disturbing vision of her dead husband. We cannot possibly imagine the further pain this unenviable task had on Rose and the sight she had witnessed, something which would remain with her for the rest of her life as it did with Alec Ward whom I am reliably informed by the Ward family, never got over the experience of discovering Bill's lifeless body. Rose returned home with Agnes and Frank a broken woman, still numb with grief and yet to face the daunting prospect of the approaching funeral, planned for Saturday the 1st of October.

The day after Bill's murder, Bishop Inskip asked the Rev. Armitage, who broke the news of the murder to Rose if he would be willing to take part in the funeral subject to the agreement of Rose and the family. The Rev. Armitage paid Rose another caring visit to seek her thoughts and approval on the suggestions made by the bishop with the tearful and grieving Rose nodding in agreement to his words. The Rev. Armitage also asked Rose if she would like words to be said at the graveside delicately explaining that the assembled mourners, police representatives and friends may expect this but emphasised to Rose that this would only be carried out at her discretion.

The Rev. Armitage telephoned the bishop to explain in relieved and positive terms how Rose had agreed to his suggestions; a letter promptly being sent to the Reverend Roberts, the Vicar of Christchurch to brief him on the compassionate funeral service arrangements suggested by the bishop.

Agnes Cross suggested to Rose that the funeral could be held from her house at 58 Junction Road in Warley, Brentwood where George's body, now having been respectfully prepared and dressed for its last journey by the established family firm, Bennett's Undertakers of Warley, had arrived and was placed in an open coffin in the flower- and wreath-adorned front room where an almost endless procession of police officers from all over the country filed through to silently pay their respects to their fallen comrade.

The black-edged memorial card produced for Bill Gutteridge.

Courtesy of, Mr Brian Alexander

The day of the funeral was cloudy with a steady rain falling from the leaden skies as a large group from Stapleford Abbotts and some surrounding villages had prepared for the sombre journey across country to Warley Hill, Brentwood to witness what was to be a hero's funeral with full honours and of huge proportions, the like of which was only reserved for those in high office and senior members of the armed forces. An occasion rare in this part of the country.

Most of the people from the villages made their way on foot in a broken procession which was almost resemblant of a pilgrimage to pay their last respects to Bill Gutteridge. They made this journey to acknowledge that his determination to protect the village and its people he had 'adopted', had ultimately cost him his life, but through the manner of his death, Bill had really shown his true grit as the consummate village 'Bobby' and I would speculate, that past adversaries and critics may have now seen him in a different light and secretly compared their own level of bravery to that of Bill Gutteridge?

The polished black hearse, gracefully pulled by two beautiful plumed black horses followed by carriages containing members of the immediate family, arrived promptly at the Cross family home in Junction Road at

2.20pm from where Bill would make his final journey. Six policemen from the Ongar and Epping Division; PCs Taylor (the last police colleague to have seen and spoken to Bill Gutteridge), Sangster, Bridges, Probitts, Cook and Austin had been appointed as pall bearers and were led by Sergeant Wiseman throughout the sad ceremony.

The coffin, with Police Comrades as bearers, leaving the house at Brentwood for the church.

Colleagues including PC Sydney Taylor on the right carrying Bill's coffin from the Cross family home in Junction Road to the waiting hearse.

Courtesy of the Sunday News, 2nd October 1927

They respectfully carried Bill's wreath-adorned coffin to the waiting hearse with the agonisingly distraught Rose joining her sister Agnes, her husband Frank and daughter Olive in the following carriages. Little Jack however, cried so bitterly at seeing his mother so upset, he had to be comforted by friends who remained behind with him at the Cross family home whilst the funeral proceeded but took him along later to the churchyard to see the burial and closing scenes of the touching proceedings; an experience no child of his age should have to witness.

The funeral cortege moved respectfully and almost silently along crowded flower-lined lanes towards its final destination of Christchurch in Warley, the roads almost congested with friends, many in tears and sobbing, onlookers and supporters whose communities had been rocked by Bill's murder most notably the large group of mourners from the village Bill had tenaciously defended to the end; Stapleford Abbotts. These supportive villagers were very appropriately and deservedly given a special place in the procession almost as a regiment of soldiers march as one in a show of pride and solidarity for their lost guardian.

The *Essex Chronicle* soberly and accurately reported the list of family mourners as:

Rose Gutteridge, (Widow), Muriel Gutteridge, (Daughter), Mrs M. Edwards, (Mother), Mr and Mrs F. Cross, (Brother-in-law and Sister-in-law), Mr and Mrs J Gutteridge of West Ham, (Uncle and Aunt), Mr H Gutteridge of Barrington, (Uncle), Mrs C. Gutteridge of Downham Market, (Aunt), Mr Arthur Savill, (Brother-in-law), Mr Cecil Savill of Newmarket, (Brother-in law), Mrs A Savill, (Sister-in-law), PC and Mrs Meadows of Braintree, (Brother-in-law and Sister-in-law), Mr Mrs Rawlinson of March, (Brother in law, Sister-in law)

And from the small community of Stapleford Abbotts:

W. Edward, Ernest Viney, Jack Sayward, Mrs Quilter, Mrs Dennis,

Mrs Alexander, Mr, Mrs and Miss Sutton, Nurse Jarman, Distict Nurse at Stapleford Abbotts and Nurse Barrett, District Nurse at Lambourne End

with many more unreported names in attendance.

The level of respect awarded to PC George William Gutteridge that relentlessly rainy and mainly overcast day in Warley was very evident as during the funeral the whole neighbourhood had fallen silent with many businesses and public life being suspended for the duration with blinds on houses being drawn as used to be the custom, being a very visual mark of respect for the deceased with flags on important buildings flying at half mast. There is no exaggeration here and to document the local, national and international representation of police forces and many other organisations in respect of Bill Gutteridge and abhorrence of his needless murder would certainly occupy several chapters in its own right.

Long before the funeral service had commenced, the public gallery inside Christchurch had, not unexpectedly, been filled to capacity with two thirds of the other seating in the church, (ably planned and stewarded by the churchwardens Mr A. Cumbers, Mr H.G. Camp and Mr Copland), being occupied by many senior police officers representing their own regional forces. They waited in silent and sombre anticipation of the arrival of the hearse and funeral cortege. Warley, a growing Brentwood town, had rarely witnessed anything like this with a complement of over 200 policemen marching in front of and behind the funeral cortege.

The funeral procession marches up Warley Hill

A brief ray of sunshine shines on Bill's coffin and the guard of honour
as it is about to enter Christchurch.

Images (X3) Courtesy of the Essex Police Museum and the Sunday News, 2nd October 1927

This show of strength and support comprised representatives of police forces up and down the country who, at the end of the journey up Warley Hill and on the approach to Christchurch would form a guard of honour to their fallen comrade PC George William Gutteridge of the Essex County Constabulary.

Christchurch was completed in March 1855, the product of a great drive by the then Rector of Warley village, The Reverend Dr Hastings Robinson to establish a 'beacon of godliness' in what he referred to as a 'gaping spiritual void' which now existed in this fast-growing town.

The imposing building of Christchurch, Great Warley.

Picture by author
Courtesy of Christchurch Warley

The wonderful and welcoming interior of Christchurch facing the chancel steps
where Dr Inskip delivered his address.

Picture by author
Courtesy of Christchurch Warley

Warley, being host to approximately 50 pubs, a military barracks, the very large Essex County Lunatic Asylum and the arrival of a mainline railway station many years previously in 1840, it is easy to imagine that this once quiet area of Essex was fast becoming more multicultural and cosmopolitan, now inexorably linked to the great metropolis of London and other major cities through the expanding mainline railway network.

Now, the spotlight would fall on Christchurch as it hosted a hero's funeral in the most tragic of circumstances with 200 policemen standing solemnly inside and in anticipation of the arrival of the coffin containing their late colleague whilst outside in the unrelenting rain, standing dutifully to attention stood the guard of honour flanking the approach and entrance to the church. The Vicar of Christchurch at the time was the Reverend Lewelyn Cradock Roberts MA, who previously had made preparations for the order of service as suggested by the bishop.

The Right Reverend Dr James Theodore Inskip.

Courtesy of an unknown artist, National Portrait Gallery

Dr James Inskip (pictured), a fellow of Ridley Hall Theological College Cambridge, was a great philanthropist and humanitarian, a true ambassador of his Christian faith illustrated throughout by his active and continued support for the now widowed Rose and her family whose uncertain future now hung in the balance.

The late Arthur Bennett, founder of Bennetts Funeral Services of Brentwood led the flower and wreath adorned black hearse pulled by 2 black plumed horses as it moved slowly away from the Cross family home in Junction road at precisely 2.20 pm, preceded by a large detachment of police officers marching in line until it gracefully drew to a halt outside Christchurch Warley for the funeral service at 2.30pm.

Courtesy of Bennett's Funeral Directors, Brentwood, Essex.

Standing huddled in the rain, the hundreds of mourners many having arrived on foot from Stapleford Abbotts and surrounding villages waited silently and respectfully observing a respectful silence with heads bowed, faces displaying sadness, tears mingling with the rain and disbelief as the pall bearers, comprising close colleagues of Bill Gutteridge slowly and purposefully carried his wreath-laden coffin in through the side doorway of the church, the funeral party having been met upon arrival by the Reverend James William Armitage as it approached Christchurch.

The wreath-bedecked coffin was closely but respectfully followed by the tearful, distraught and pathetic-looking Rose Gutteridge with her daughter Muriel carrying a posy of chrysanthemums which she would later drop onto her father's coffin during the graveside ceremony of committal. Rose was continually supported in her grief by her cousin Olive Cross as they walked with arms around each other's shoulders and together clutching a large umbrella, with Rose's sisters and Mary Edwards, Bill's grieving mother following close behind as the funeral party entered the church.

Mr H.J. Andrews the church organist played respectful and appropriate entry music as family and friends quietly processed in and took their seats, Rose Gutteridge with eyes closed and her face ashen, almost in a state of collapse had to be helped to her seat by her very close and supportive sister Agnes and her husband, Frank Cross. The Vicar of Christchurch, the Reverend Llewellyn Cradock Roberts respectfully and positively opened the funeral service followed by the Rev. Armitage reading Psalm 39 after which, prayers were said.

Mr Andrews then played the first beautifully worded and uplifting hymn *Jesus, Lover of my Soul* by Charles Wesley which was reported to have been sung 'very impressively' by the assembled congregation. A heartrending thing to witness as was illustrated in the *Sunday News* the next day, October the 2nd 1927. The church was full, mostly with police officers. The gathered masses of mourners and friends standing outside the church in respectful silence in the unremitting rain as the funeral service proceeded inside; sadly unable to hear the prayers and dedication to the life of Bill Gutteridge. (Unlike the computerised and sophisticated public address systems often used today to 'include' the general public and supporters in high profile ceremonies such was the case (without comparison) at the funeral of Princess Diana at Westminster Abbey, lest they deny the tearful assembly of outside mourners of their right as citizens to be part of such a public outpouring of grief.)

During the service Bishop Inskip stood on the chancel steps to address the congregation and during his lengthy and forthright address, took full opportunity to commend the bravery, courage and tenacity of PC Gutteridge in pursuit of his duty without thought for himself, addressing the transfixed silent congregation comprised mostly of policemen saying, 'he might probably have saved himself if he had chosen, but that would not have been true to the traditions of the force or of himself'; reinforcing this further in reference to the obvious courage of Bill Gutteridge and of Christian teaching, 'he had to face his cross alone; not an easy thing to do'. 1(*See footnote below.*)

However, Bishop Inskip was not regarded as a 'fire and brimstone' preacher, his 'simmering' but passionate delivery exuding much more power in this exceptional set of circumstances and using his address to great effect in attacking and questioning the 'masculinity'and 'Englishness' of the perpetrators of this terrible and very deliberate murder. His admirable restraint and carefully controlled emotions evident in the words he expressed in forthright terms in condemning the cowardly actions of the still as yet, unidentified killer or killers referring to them saying, 'They must be desperado's; men without hope'. He also compared their actions with that of uncivilised tribes

---

1 **Footnote:** author's view

I consider that this is a very astute and concise description by the Bishop Inskip of the strong and tenacious character George Gutteridge developed, possibly as a product of his hardship and early experiences of life without a father figure?

in remote parts of the world with little regard for life; going on to question rhetorically if the perpetrators were, indeed Englishmen and lamenting that this kind of disregard for life and the law, was sadly on the increase.

It could be argued that Dr Inskip's style of delivery and choice of words were effectively 'throwing down the gauntlet' to the perpetrators to surrender themselves for this dastardly crime but in doing so, this must have intentionally, or by effect, provided a significant boost to the determination of those present at the service in apprehending the killers, not just to the representatives of the assembled police forces, but also in appealing to the nation to join the now nationwide manhunt which was growing in intensity and momentum.

Although supported by close family with Muriel and Olive and Mrs Edwards sitting only a few feet from the coffin containing her husband, the emotional strain Rose was suffering became too much for her, suddenly becoming overwhelmed with grief, collapsing into the arms of her sister Agnes (Peg) during the service but Nurse Jarman, the District Nurse at Stapleford Abbotts sitting nearby in the congregation, quickly hurried to Rose's side to provide medical assistance whilst the young Muriel dressed from head to toe in black cut a pathetic figure sitting still in a tearful state of shock with her cousin Olive closely supporting her. As the funeral service came to a close, Mr Andrews played another appropriately chosen hymn, *O' Rest in the Lord* as the congregation stood and the pall bearers assembled preparing to take Bill on his last journey to Christchurch Cemetery and to say a final goodbye to her husband at the emotional commitment service at the graveside.

Rose Gutteridge Bids a Final Farewell to her Husband

Bill's coffin was taken by the waiting hearse in respectful procession continually overseen by Arthur Bennett to the ancient and established Christchurch Lawns Cemetery (now Lorne Road Cemetery, pictured).

A rare and poor quality image of the hearse having stopped with Bill's colleagues respectfully carrying the coffin to its last destination only a few yards away with the distraught Muriel and her cousin Olve Cross, touchingly with arms around each other in support.

Courtesy, the Essex Chronicle, October 7th 1927

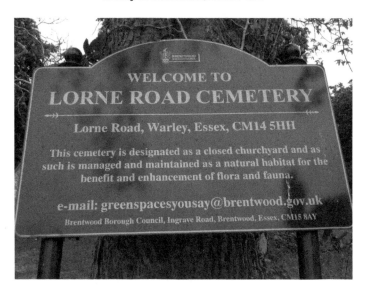

Above, the entrance sign to the old cemetery at Lorne Road Warley. This calm and now closed cemetery serving as a peaceful and valuable conservation area in the bustling area of Brentwood.

Picture by Author

The old disused chapel of Christchurch Cemetery, Lorne Road Warley.

Picture by author

The Interment and the Reading of the Last Rites.

Courtesy of the Essex Police Museum, Chelmsford

With full police honours, Police Constable 218 George William Gutteridge of the Essex County Constabulary was interred with all due ceremony in public grave No. B131, the last to be excavated, which had previously been checked and approved by the forward thinking and astute gravediggers to ensure this plot would not only accommodate Bill's coffin but that of Rose in the many years to follow.

A large gathering of mourners, clergy and police stood respectfully together including the Chief Constable Captain J. A. Unett in military dress uniform, the Reverend Llewellyn Cradock Roberts, Vicar of Christchurch, displaying the medals he was awarded for service in the Great War stood to attention and saluted Bill's coffin. Together with the Reverend James Armitage they conducted the last rites. Rose, carrying a floral harp with broken strings was then brought forward to view her husband's coffin for the last time but as she stood transfixed in disbelief she let her floral harp descend into the grave as her final and loving, parting gesture as she stood . gazing surreally at her husband's coffin. Friends came to lead her away but she resisted briefly before falling limply into the arms of those around her as poor Muriel, with her cousin Olive both crying piteously let her bouquet of chrysanthemums fall onto her father's already flower-covered coffin.

As the family mourners withdrew it was reported that an hour passed as people filed past the grave to pay their last respects to PC Bill Gutteridge.

Still Keeping Watch

The strikingly well-maintained grave of PC George Gutteridge thanks to the care and attention paid to it by members of his family, distinct and proud in the new conservation environment at Lorne Road, Warley.

Picture by author

The 'ripple' effect of the bishop's address emboldened and enhanced the vigilance of people who, in their daily lives were now highly motivated and wishing to help in finding clues to this dreadful murder. As can be seen from the fine example below, a copy of the actual telephone message sent to the Chief Constable only three days after the funeral of PC Gutteridge after a road fund licence in a metal holder was found and handed to Loughton Police Station by Sir Joseph Lowry of Loughton.

ESSEX COUNTY CONSTABULARY.

FORM No. 101.
Division.
Station.
4th October, 19 27.

TELEPHONE MESSAGE.

From Supt. Hicks, Hackney.   To Chief Constable,
Clissold 0200.   Chelmsford

Despatched at   Received at
By   By D.C.C.

At 8.15 a.m. 3rd October, 1927, Sir Joseph Lowry of the Hermitage, Loughton, deposited at Loughton Station a road fund licence in metal holder No. 0790581 assigned to a Citroen bus private motor car Index No. N.O.782 issued by Essex County Council, 30th March, 1927, expiring 31st December, 1927. Sir Joseph stated that he found the licence by the side of the road at Theydon Mount Road whilst motoring at 12 noon the 2nd October, 1927 and as the spot was within about a mile or so of the scene of the murder of the late P.C. Gutteridge he thought it might have some bearing on the case.

forwarded for xxxxx information. of Supt. Attridge.
—McO. & Co. Ltd., Ldn.—   the

Courtesy of the Essex Police Museum Chelmsford

This represents a prime example of vigilance in the search for clues by a stalwart member of the public, Sir Joseph Lowry and although this proved to be unconnected with the murder it just goes to prove that no stone was being left unturned in the search for the killers.

On the 6th October 1927 shortly after the funeral Rose wrote a very kind and graceful letter of thanks and acknowledgement from the home of her sister Agnes Cross in Junction Road Warley where she was staying, to the Chief Constable Captain Unett and his wife which reads:

To, The Chief Constable of Essex.

Dear Sir:
It is with my heartfull of gratitude, that I wish to send my sincere thanks to Mrs Unett and yourself, for the sympathy, kindness, and attention I have received from both of you, in connection with the distressful tragedy which has shrouded the future life of myself, and my 2 children.

And I also send my heartfelt thanks to yourself, officers, Non.Com. Officers and men of the Essex County Constabulary for all ranks at,

Chadwell Heath Police Station
K Div. Metropolitan Police
LNER Police Station E section: London Division
Tilbury Docks
M Div. of the Metrolpolitan Police
Grays Division

I am Sir
Yours most respectfully:
Mrs Gutteridge and Family

The Drive to Support Rose and Her Children Begins in Earnest

In the interim, Dr Inskip lost little time in launching what was to be known as the 'Bishop's Fund'; his status and title giving the appeal gravitas in the appeal for financial help for Rose and the children with a suggested figure of £100. By the 21st October 1927 £16 .13 shillings was raised from private donations. Churches such as St. Barnabus Church, Walthamstow raised 10 shillings from a 'score of churchmen' referring to this as 'a slight expression' with St. Saviours Church, also of Walthamstow raising 15 shillings through donations or 'mites' as they were then called, including the sum of £2 from Lord Lambourne of Stapleford Abbotts who commended PC George Gutteridge by expressing in a letter that, 'he found him; [PC Gutteridge] to be the most painstaking and capable officer and worthy of the great force of which he was a member', here representing another consummate example expressed by a Lord of the manor of the dedication to duty Bill Gutteridge was known for and by the criminal element, despised.

Concurrent with the 'Bishop's Fund', the *Chelmsford Chronicle* set their own fundraising initiative entitled the 'Widow's Fund' which by Friday the 4th November 1927 announced that £46.17s.1d had been raised; appealing further stating with some urgency that 'Fund for the Policeman's Widow and Children £53.2s.11d still required to meet the target of £100'. By Friday the 18th November the amount raised increased to £78.10s.7d and by Friday of the next week, (the day the paper was published), the figure had risen to £88.15s. 6d demonstrating the strong public support shown for Rose and her children.

Archived evidence shows that many organisations including national newspapers were willing to launch fundraising initiatives in support of Rose which could have eased further her burden of grief and re-housing crisis immensely but this was not to be. The bishop, realising the great value of these offers of help shown by the *Chelmsford Chronicle* in addition to his own 'Bishop's Fund' in providing Rose with a little security must have been quite enthused but then surprised and somewhat 'deflated' by the polite but assertive letter he received from the Chief Constable, Capt. Unett dated the 4th October 1927 (only three days after the funeral of PC Gutteridge) in which he appears to wish to limit fundraising initiatives in support of Rose and her children.

The original letter reads:

4th October 1927

My Dear Bishop,

I think I am correct in saying that Mrs Gutteridge has no private means whatever. An opportunity will be given her, which she may wish to accept, to send one or more of her two children to the Police School free of charge. She will receive about £40 from the Police Insurance fund and the pension which will be payable to her and her two children amount to £109. 9. 11. Per annum.*

She is in no immediate want for money because my Superintendents and I are advancing paying her money until such time as the pension to which she is entitled is paid.

I should be extremely reluctant to say or do anything which might be construed as putting any obstacle in the way of a fund being raised for her benefit and were such a fund started by any newspaper I am sure there would be a prompt and generous reply to it, but at the same time it must be appreciated that the public are in fact paying her a pension for life and that the Police School will, I know, take her children.

If any such fund were raised I should like to see it restricted to about £100, which would enable her to pay off any existing debts and move comfortably into another house.

Yours sincerely,

(Signature of Capt. Unett)
Chief Constable of Essex

*The pension to the children (15. 10. 0. each) is included in the above and ceases at 16 years of age. In the event of the children entering the Police School the childrens pension would be paid to the School Authorities.

This is in stark contrast compared to the case of the brutal murder of Sergeant Eves in the previous century, when the large sum of £400 was raised for his widow through public subscription as the police widow's pension awarded to her then was described as being 'miserly' by the public.

Despite the less than compassionate letter the bishop received from the Chief Constable, the undertaker's bill would still have to be met by Rose out of the £40 police insurance money she was to receive and accounted for over a half of this sum which amounted to £22 . 8 shillings. Capt. Unett wrote to Colonel Scott of the National Police Fund requesting that a *limited* amount (£10) be provided for this purpose and boldly overriding this limitation, Colonel Scott wrote to Capt Unett on the 1st November 1927 saying;

Dear Capt. Unett,

I have received your letter of the 31st instant and I write to say that it has been decided to pay the whole of the undertakers bill for Mrs Gutteridge.

I therefore enclose a cheque for £22.8.0 on account of the funeral expenses in connection with Mrs Gutteridge's late husband;

Sincerely yours,
Col Scott.

Rose characteristically wrote a heart wrenching and very touching letter to acknowledge this very kind gesture to Police Sergeant 31.

Marriage, Secretary, Joint Branch Board of the National Police Fund, Canvey Island on the 12th November 1927 from her home at 102, Victoria Street, Braintree;

Dear Sir,

Your very kind letter received, and it is with my heart full of gratitude that I desire to express my sincere thanks to the members of the Essex Constabulary, the members of the branch board meeting, Norfolk Constabulary, Caernarvonshire Constabulary and Liverpool City which you have the hounour to represent, for their very touching expressions of sympathy and condolence in my very sudden and cruel bereavement. The sympathy bestwed upon myself and my children by the police of all forces throughout this most distressing time, which has shrouded the future life of myself and my children, has been of the most generous, respectful and sympathetic nature and beyond my power to answer individually and I ask if you would be so kind as to convey my thanks and gratitude to those you have the honour to represent and with pride and admiration their kind and comforting words, will impress upon my memory a lasting appreciation to the police forces throughout England in my sad endeavor to bear my cross alone.

Yours sincerely,
Mrs R A E Gutteridge

The press continued to pester Rose for her life story but again in her dignity she refused. Muriel Alexander in later years is quoted as saying that 'what went in the papers was not what she'd told them'. This is evident in the sensational and purely fictional account of a 'dream or vision' in which Rose supposedly had had, concocted by a journalist which appeared in the *Sunday News* of the 2nd October (the day after the funeral), in which it reports that Rose had said to them that she had dreamt that she saw three men in the car her policeman husband George had stopped, who each played a part in the murder further giving 'clear' descriptions of them and what they were wearing; the leader of these criminals encouraging the other two to take turns to shoot so making the trio equally guilty of the killing and even quoting the leader as saying 'come on, we must all be in it'. This was pure fabrication and sensationalism by a representative of a national newspaper seemingly devoid of any compassion or regard for the feelings for a very publicly widowed Rose Gutteridge. So convincing was the article published by the *Sunday News* to a wide readership that it came to the attention of Superintendent Wood who understandably was still investigating all and any possible leads to identifying the killers. He spoke to Rose who, still very upset in her raw state of grief, told Superintendent Wood, who stated in his letter to the Chief Constable;

> With regard to the paragraph appearing in the 'Sunday News' newspaper of the 2nd instant, (2nd October) Mrs Gutteridge informs me that the whole of it relating to her alleged dream and interview are untrue and that she is consulting a solicitor on the matter tomorrow.

> Wood,
> Superintendent

It is unclear whether Rose pursued this blatant mis-representation of her comments or could even have afforded to, but I would suggest that this fictional, unhelpful and large feature would have drawn condemnation from the authorities who were still avidly seeking the real truth in this ongoing murder enquiry. In the early aftermath of the murder whilst a huge nationwide manhunt was still in progress, estimated at nine thousand policemen, plus other agencies, the general public and genuine offers of help from a wide section of the community, police enquiries were continuing to pour in with members of the public and press maintaining a vigil-like presence around Romford Police Station, the centre of the investigation, in the hope of gaining some news.

But a wave of excitement grew and sensation was caused when it became known that the police had a man in custody although his arrival had not been noticed (understandably, as at this time the suspect was still in police custody in Basingstoke).

This burly and unkempt man gave his name as 24-year-old Andrew Baldwing from Basingstoke in Hampshire who it transpired had heard of the murder in the national press and decided to surrender himself to a beat Constable at the market place in Basingstoke for the murder of PC Gutteridge. He had done so previously for another gruesome murder using the alias 'Mr Beattie', in London earlier that year known as the Trunk Murder in which a young woman was killed, dismembered and her body parts forced into a trunk which found its way into the left luggage office at Charing Cross railway station where it remained for five days and only opened when the terrible stench of the decomposing body became unbearable. The real killer, John Robinson of London was subsequently convicted and hanged for the murder of Minnie Bonati, a part-time prostitute.

Baldwing had been taken into custody and made a very convincing and detailed statement to Hampshire Police in which he stated that he had been riding along the Romford to Ongar road in the early hours of Tuesday morning, the 27th September, when PC Gutteridge had stopped him for having no lights on his bike. Baldwin stated that 'words followed and then I let him have it'. He then allegedly stated that he had thrown the revolver away and would show the police where it was. Detectives, under the firm hand of Chief Inspector Berrett of Scotland Yard who was directing the case, took Baldwin discreetly and out of sight of the press back to Romford Police Station, the designated centre of enquiries, for further questioning where his statements would be investigated in closer detail.

Intensive questioning followed and he remained in custody overnight. As apprehension grew, the awaiting press and public, holding their breaths in anticipation for an announcement that the killer had been caught were to be disappointed and very deflated in the high expectations they now held of a front page 'scoop' as the police, after extensive and intensive enquiries, announced to the waiting press and public that there was no foundation to Baldwin's claim to be the killer and he was discreetly released, to the frustration of the press and public and disgust of those officers whose valuable time and resources had been effectively wasted by this sadly common false admission of guilt. This deranged and no doubt mentally ill individual who, along with others of the same ilk wrote to newspapers with similar admissions and voyeuristic fantasy accounts of the murder exacerbated the situation further by people sending parcels containing guns and ammunition to the police and press.

Items such as these 'planted' by strange individuals simply hindered and confused the hunt for the murderers who were now further and further away and still prolifically committing further crimes as is documented in *The Trial of Browne and Kennedy*.

Rose Gutteridge, even in her fragile state, had appealed before the funeral for any information and was reported as saying in the *News of the World* the next day on October 2nd and quoted by Dr Chipperfield, who states that they [the *News of the World*] reportedly claimed that Rose Gutteridge had told them that 'her husband had often spoken to her of the danger along the lonely roads he patrolled because of the increase of motor bandits abroad at night' allegedly going on to say that 'often he reported the presence in the district of suspicious characters, and told her shortly before the tragedy that he was keeping a sharp lookout for one particular gang'. Could this have been a further example of sensationalism by the press? Or even true, we will never know.

Rose also found herself being drawn, but willingly, into the investigation and reported to the police that she had been told by another, that a man had been seen buying a revolver from a shop in Brentwood High Street three days before the murder of her husband, such was the huge public determination to find the killers and to use a contemporary term; 'the hunt had gone viral'. The police wasted no time in following this up and found that a young man, later traced, had visited a shop called Price's in Brentwood High Street to look at a Browning automatic pistol out of 'idle curiosity' but without posessing a firearms licence he could not purchase it. Newspapers such as the *News of the World* continued to offer large rewards; initially £1000 later to be increased to £2000 to identify the killers resulting from a still very raw public outcry, such was the public abomination of this crime. This offer of a considerable reward of course predictably attracted people who considered that they were entitled to the large reward including an unemployed sailor, Joseph Dyson of Gravesend in Kent who, months later on the 29th April 1928 with the killers now in custody and awaiting trial, brimming with self-importance wrote an untidy, bizarre, misspelt four page roughly written and blotched with ink, foolscap letter to the Chief Constable outlining his entitlement to the reward, the main points of which have been summarised within context in this piece.

Self-appointed to unofficially represent the taxpayers of Essex but with an obvious agenda, Dyson stated to Capt. Unett that the cost of the case has so far amounted to £5000 with Essex ratepayers bearing the cost. (How he calculated this is a mystery and probably based on assumption.) He states that he had also written to the King, {George V}, saying that if the statement he sent to Inspector Berrett had been acted upon 'the case could have been cleared up long ago and the cost halved', further indicating that he had had a reply from the King's secretary stating that his letter had been transmitted to the Home Secretary for an enquiry.

Inspector Berrett later told Dyson that he was not entitled to the reward as the police were already aware of the activities and identity of

Browne and Kennedy and that Dyson had not elaborated positively, providing no further evidence on the murder of PC Gutteridge. Inspector Berrett told the *News of The World* on the 28th April 1927 that the ex-convict who had been working with Browne and Kennedy, (also named Dyson, although any connection is unclear and not appropriate to this work), had been of great assistance in the murder enquiry. Dyson's rambling letter pleads with Capt. Unett to intercede to the Home Secretary about his claim to the reward of £2000 (over £116,000 today) heavily criticising the formidable and legendary thorough work of Inspector Berrett with his close and very experienced team of investigators and implying further that the informant had been forced to give evidence under duress, stating on page 3 of his letter that: 'this ex-convict is not entitled to any reward as he is an accessory to the fact and *might* have been in the car at the time of the murdur [sic]'. The implication is interesting and no doubt was investigated by Inspector Berrett. Dyson's arrogance is evident in the conclusion of his letter to Capt. Unett in which he says; 'If you would care for an interview I shall be pleased to come and see you as I am at present unemployed [sic]', *Joseph Dyson.*

The activities of this meddling individual even at this late stage were counter productive, adding unneccesary complications and work to the still very active police investigations which had been fruitless with one frustrating 'dead end' after another. But despite the efforts of some who attempted to divert the enquiry either inadvertantly or those with a hidden agenda, were in the main, people from all walks of life and were genuine in their efforts to help. Such was the willingness of people in society to help, even a professional medium from Wales made himself available to assist in the search using his psychic powers but it is unclear if he was taken up on his offer. The magnitude of the hunt could not be overstated, such was the affront, indignation and disgust felt by the wider population resulting from this needless murder.

With some difficulty, Stapleford Abbotts was attempting to return to some form of normality with life going on as before to some extent, but as Margaret Sutton explained to me, the village community became much closer, more vigilant and supportive of each other, in a similar way to the Neighbourhood Watch schemes of today, being very distrustful and wary of 'strangers' who visited the village as there was still an air of fear and danger present as the killers had not yet been caught with some members of the community understandably thinking the murderer or murderers may be in their midst and possibly ready to strike again. As is well documented, this proved not to be the case but the public reaction of fear to this sudden and brutal murder is completely understandable as can be imagined.

People would no longer leave their doors open as they had done previously for neighbours to pay unannounced and occasional visits to share news, to see if their neighbours were OK or to borrow some milk or sugar for instance. Now the windows and doors remained firmly locked, especially at night, fearing a visit from an unknown and still on the run, killer of their village policeman.

But for poor Rose and her children, life would and never could, be the same again with many more challenges and hardships which would have to be faced, as events subsequently portrayed. Given the wonderful support of the Alexander and Cross families, friends and relatives, Rose did her best to carry on, always putting her children before herself including going without food to ensure they had enough to eat as the late Muriel Alexander explained in later years further saying of Rose, 'I had a good mother, and she wouldn't remarry in any case, and she never had any men friends'. As can be imagined, this particular Christmas in 1927 for the Gutteridges was devoid of the normal joy and excitement it would normally hold for the hub of the family but again Rose's sister Agnes (Peg) and her family most probably gave hope and support to Rose and the children by making this particular Christmas as good as it could be in the circumstances.

CHAPTER 12

JANUARY 1928 AND AN UNANNOUNCED INTRUSION

One day in January 1928 there was knock at the door and young Muriel rushed to open it, as her mother was in the back garden, to find a tall young policeman and a young woman standing there. Without the courtesy of polite introduction, this policeman announced to Muriel that 'he would be living there' and proceeded to walk into the house without invitation. This was 28-year-old PC 470 Robert Merchant who had left industry as a ships plater to join the Essex Constabulary in 1925, accompanied by his fiancée, Frances Irene. He was to be the village replacement to Bill Gutteridge and posted there by his superiors both to 'fill a vacancy' and to announce his presence and intentions to the Gutteridge family.

As can be imagined, his sudden arrival without any prior notice from the authorities to Rose (research does not confirm this), came as quite a shock to Rose, made worse by this tall stranger telling young Muriel, a vulnerable and now frightened child who had recently lost her loving father, that he was coming to live in her house. This was a very regrettable invasion into the only personal sanctuary a recently bereaved and grieving young family possessed. This could be construed as 'constructive eviction' but this tough Cambridgeshire girl was not going to be bullied out of her own home. This sudden incursion did not enamour Rose to her soon-to-be new joint occupiers who, having invited themselves in, seemed to lack compassion for a widow's plight and as will be illustrated later, a lack of respect for the cottage Rose had lovingly maintained.

The now newly married PC and Mrs Robert Merchant took up residence at 2 Towneley Cottages on the 15th February 1928 having been allocated two rooms; a bedroom and the other to be used as a sitting room with all the other facilities ie; cooking, washing, heating, toilet, etc, to be used on a 'shared' basis with Rose Gutteridge and her children.

I think it fair to state that from the outset Rose understandably objected very strongly, giving her new joint-tenants a very frosty reception to their unwanted but officially sanctioned presence and within days it was clear that this imposed arrangement which resulted in a lifestyle and social clash was doomed to fail with Rose and the Merchants 'crossing swords' on many early and subsequent occasions as is evident in archived reports.

Rose was a very fastidious woman having lost her mother at an early age and then her elder sister Christina, when she was away in service. She was not house proud in the extreme sense but perhaps for her, and typical of the period, many working-class women regarded that their home (as most still do) as *their* domain while their husbands worked. Most took their responsibilities seriously having great pride in maintaining a regular routine and regime in acting as the 'keeper of their household' and looking after the children. But this represented much more to Rose who had created an oasis for her children and herself, a refuge and place of safety which had been unceremoniously invaded. Rose never 'buried her head in the sand', so to speak, about eventually having to move from Towneley Cottages, being all too aware that police accommodation was only provided for serving officers and their families in the community in which they worked but she was a determined lady and would leave when she found a place to live. From this point on Rose was on her own to fend for herself.

With George now gone, Rose had written to Superintendent Wood regarding a house for rent at Hutton she hoped to get. Inspector

Poulson had followed this up for Rose to be told by Superintendent Wood that the house had been let. Although disappointed, this illustrates that Rose had been proactive in seeking accommodation for herself and the children rather than relying on the police to do this and as is known they did less than what could have been achieved to lessen the hardship Rose faced.

But why was Rose cast adrift with a young family? Was it because she declined the offer to place her children in the police orphanage and therefore fragment her family? It seems that this was a cold hearted 'take it or leave it' option offered to her by Essex County Constabulary but Rose fought it admirably. Questions still hang in the air all these years later as to why she had to find her own way and endure much hardship considering that her late husband now had hero status. A very sad indictment of the way the police authorities treated the widow of a very brave policeman in 1927. It is appropriate again to refer here to the murder of Sergeant Eves as there are parallels to be drawn in the way his widow was left to endure financial austerity in comparison with the hardship Rose Gutteridge suffered.

John Woodgate stated in his book *The Essex Police*, 1985 that; 'Mrs Eves was awarded the highest pension permitted at the time, £15 a year, whereupon a public subscription was organised which raised £400, echoing it was said, "the disgust of the people at the miserly provision made for such incidents".'

The late Muriel Alexander is quoted as saying gracefully 'that's how things were then'. As time went on, the *joint* domestic situation at the police cottage deteriorated further almost to breaking point with Frances Merchant issuing an ultimatum to her husband that, unless he made an application to be relocated to another station, she said that she would make her own arrangements to move out. Robert Merchant wasted no time in composing his application for fear of being parted from his new wife. Merchant composed a lengthy, pleading letter to his immediate superior, Sgt. Wiseman requesting a change of station indicating that in his desperation he would, if necessary make this application to the Chief Constable, Capt. Unett himself if his initial request was rejected.

He went on to write in desperate terms that he was struggling to live there any longer in the very tense situation, apportioning the blame on Rose Gutteridge for unreasonable and deliberately obstructive behaviour saying that the situation had affected his wife's health to the point of illness.

Recognising the gravity of this as an unworkable and potentially explosive situation, Sgt. Wiseman needed to act in the current climate of public support for the recently widowed Rose Gutteridge. Sgt. Wiseman immediately forwarded this letter to Inspector Poulton on the 26th March 1928, just over a month after the Merchants had moved in.

Inspector Poulson went to Towneley Cottages to assess the situation for himself and following his visit, compiled a report on his findings to the Chief Constable. This report, dated the 27th March 1928 states that Inspector Poulson visited Towneley Cottages and spoke with PC and Mrs Merchant who confirmed what had been written in the letter to Sgt. Wiseman. He then put this to Rose Gutteridge who said that she had never prevented them from using the kitchen and had 'actually tried' to help by always lighting a fire to provide hot water for PC Merchant to shave, as his wife 'didn't get up in the morning'. Rose went on to say that Mrs Merchant had used the 'copper' in the scullery on the previous Thursday but had failed to empty it. Always precise, Inspector Poulton found this to be true. Rose further stated that she had never prevented them from using the kitchen either, despite PC Merchant stating to the contrary and that they were now forced to use oil stoves for cooking. This did not 'cut any ice' with Inspector Poulton who pointed out to Mrs Merchant that 'she had always used an oil stove and he had seen it in use when they first moved in'.

Inspector Poulton explained diplomatically to the Merchants that allowances needed to made for Mrs Gutteridge in light of her circumstances until she had found accommodation elsewhere, further stating in his report that since PC and Mrs Merchant had moved in, their rooms were far from the clean condition they were in previously, with Inspector Poulton listing a variety of things that he observed during his inspection of the cottage. He noticed that the oil stoves in the Merchants rooms were making the ceiling very black, the floor being very dirty with a heap of ashes lying on a paper in the room. On further inspection, a large tin a third full of dirty water and bedroom 'slops' was visible having been left just outside the back door of the cottage instead of being put down the toilet outside.

PC Merchant in his growing frustration then unwisely said to Inspector Poulton that 'he could not live in that pigsty' but sharp as ever, the Inspector rounded on PC Merchant suggesting that 'he could clean the floor and take the ashes out' further advising him to remove the very unhygienic slops tin saying 'it was not very nice being so close to the back door'.

Rose, wishing to contrast this situation and to further add credibility to her side of the dispute, invited Inspector Poulton into her kitchen and scullery who found these to be clean and tidy in true Rose Gutteridge tradition.

It can be seen from these accounts, sourced and quoted from original archives at the Essex Police Museum, that the allegations made by PC Merchant and his wife held little credibility with Inspector Poulson who, at first hand had witnessed evidence of how PC Merchant and his wife Irene had neglected their police accommodation, whilst being solely responsible for their own living quarters within the cottage. If they had wished to add gravity to their complaints surely would it not have been diligent to ensure their living space was clean and tidy for inspection? Inspector Poulson compiled his concerns and a graphic report was forwarded to the Chief Constable for his consideration.

It was not an idyllic or successful posting for PC Merchant and his wife with a departure from Towneley Cottages the following July.

They were posted to Grays where ironically, George and Rose were previously living and stationed.

Could it not have been possible to find Rose and her children accommodation before sending Bill's replacement to live in tandem with the Gutteridge family? I expect we will never know, but in this case any welfare provision for the bereaved family seems to be conspicuous by its virtual absence and a far cry from the support which would, no doubt, be provided by specialists in the Essex, Norfolk and other constabularies of today.

CHAPTER 13

CAST ADRIFT

Rose Gutteridge now found herself as a young woman cast aside to fend for herself and her young family. Being aware that Rose was facing severe hardship with little money and imminently no place to live, her brother-in-law PC Frank Meadows and his wife Minnie (Rose's sister) who were married at the same time in a joint ceremony, managed to find them a two-room accommodation at a house in Albert Road, Braintree, the town where George Meadows was stationed at the time.

Rose had little choice but to accept this offer and using the little money she had from collections kindly given to her by police forces from all over the country, packed up her furniture and belongings and had them transported by van to her new accommodation in Braintree.

As their cottage in Tysea Hill had been much more spacious, boasting three bedrooms upstairs in complete contrast with the previous very basic and small farmworkers' cottage at Bons Farm, they had acquired quite a lot of furniture as George was relatively well paid in comparison with many others in the essentially agricultural community of Stapleford Abbotts. Now it seemed they had regressed to below square one and to add to this sorry situation, the young Muriel was now to be parted from her neighbour and childhood sweetheart, John Alexander, not knowing when or if they would ever see each other again.

The accommodation in Albert Road Frank Meadows had kindly succeeded in getting for Rose, and very likely one of the few options available to him, proved to be wholly inadequate and verging on squalor; again, having to co-exist with minimum privacy and this time with men lodgers living on the same floor in the same house with shared sanitary facilities (the landlady preferred male lodgers as they paid more (see letter)). Muriel Alexander paints a very sad picture in her description of this house in Albert Road in describing the inadequacy of the circumstances they had to live in; having one room downstairs without an oven or sink and only an open fire with a trivet with which to cook on, so they had to survive on stewed food; hardly the balanced diet they were probably used to at Towneley Cottages.

Without a sink and proper bathing facilities the only option was to use an old tin bath in front of the fire part-filled with hot water from the kettle so everything had to be done in just this one room apart from the upstairs bedroom in which they all slept together. This was made worse as to get to the toilet, they had to walk through another common sitting room where the male lodgers congregated. Understandably, this would have been very embarrassing and inconvenient, especially for a young girl and her mother on their own.

The landlady agreed to provide them another room to store all their furniture but Rose had to pay extra for this, placing an extra burden on the very little income she had to live on and Muriel now had to attend a different school for the third time. This turned out to be good for Muriel as she now thrived and achieved much more academically than previously at the council elementary school in Havering. However, despite the cramped learning conditions of seven classes in one room her educational 'grounding' must have been effective under the stern, watchful but compassionate way in which the Head Schoolmaster, Mr Arthur Derrick and his wife (also a teacher) Clara Derrick ran and provided elementary education for the children of the village.

These people had taken an active and compassionate interest in the welfare of Rose and her children and were made aware that since the murder of her husband Bill, she had undergone continuing hardship without any support from the authorities who seemed to have 'forgotten' her and cast her adrift to fend for herself.

A Welcome Collection Benefits Two Police Widows

On the 23rd March 1928, the Joint Branch Board meeting passed a resolution at Essex Police Headquarters that a collection was to be made on the last pay day of the month throughout the force for the widows of PCs Gutteridge and Straughan, respectively of Essex and Sunderland Borough Police, and the amount raised to be equally divided. Most probably unknown to Rose whose focus now was securing another home and life for her and the children, Jane Straughan, another young woman far away in Co. Durham, who it is doubtful Rose ever met or knew of and vice-versa, had also some months before undergone a strikingly similar sudden and brutal loss of her own policeman husband Matthew (known as 'Mattie') on the fine summer evening of the 28th June 1927.

PC 464 Matthew ('Mattie') Straughan standing, his police cycle nearby,

By kind permission of Nigel Green. n.green@leedstrinity.ac.uk

PC 464 Matthew Straughan, a 36 year old tall and striking young man was married to Jane with three children, and a Constable with Sunderland Borough Police. Mattie was previously a coal miner and had served in the Royal Artilliery during the Great War enlisting as a policeman some time after.

Mattie was to issue a summons to a local man in North Hylton called Ted Lloyd; a war survivor and casualty who had suffered severe brain damage after a shell exploded near him on the Western Front had returned home after the war to his family who were housed in one of a group of derelict aerodrome huts ironically called 'Liberty Villas'. Prior to the war Ted had been a stable and strong young man and was now a mental and physical wreck as were many young men left from four years of pointless slaughter and carnage.

Unable to work, Ted's only way of earning a living was through larceny and having been caught stealing pipework from a nearby demolition site, a court appearance was on the horizon. Cycling over from Southwick Police Station to deliver a summons to Ted, PC Mattie Straughan was unaware that Lloyd was suffering, as a result of his terrible war injuries one of his frequent fits but this time his fit became worse and a deadly scenario was emerging, Ted having been seen previously by witnesses nearby to be waving a loaded shotgun around.

PC Straughan, unaware of the dangerous mental state Ted was now suffering, knocked on the door of his house to be confronted by the still deranged, 'fitting' and now furious Ted Lloyd armed with his shotgun; a man who previously it was reported was not inclined to argue. In his fury Ted aimed the gun at Mattie's face firing two shots in quick succession at very close range, the first killing him instantly with the second shot blowing away part of his hand, indicating that PC Mattie Straughan had tried to defend himself.

Lloyd was sentenced to death but a compassionate appeal for mercy by the jury to the home secretary commuted him to spending the rest of his life in a mental institution, unlike Browne and Kennedy who were conscious in their unmistakeably brutal and deliberate murder of Bill Gutteridge.

Rose now had a distant compatriot in grief and benefitted from half of the collection raised; £18. and 4 shillings. The bravery of PC Matthew Straughan was not fully recognised until 1990 when his name was entered into the Durham Constabulary Roll of Honour, curiously the same year as the roadside memorial to PC George Gutteridge was established and unveiled by the Chief Constable, John Burrow and Muriel Alexander.

Throughout this very bleak, unpleasant and unwanted interlude since the death of Bill during which the police investigation was frustrated and fruitless, Rose remained very much consumed by grief which now became compounded with growing apprehension as she had been told that the killers of her husband had been tracked down, almost by accident, resulting partly from informant help which had been given to the team investigating the murder under the tenacious and formidable, Detective Inspector James Berrett of Scotland Yard.

Frederick Guy Browne and William Henry Kennedy were now in custody and awaiting trial to which Rose suspected only too well that she would have to attend and be called as a witness to testify, another unwanted and very stressful event in her and her young family's already troubled and uncertain existence.

As is known, William Henry Kennedy had been apprehended forcefully in Liverpool on the 25th January and in the process, attempted to shoot Liverpool Detective, Sgt. Mattinson who punched Kennedy to the ground after the gun jammed, whilst some days later on the 29th Frederick Guy Browne was surrounded by police at his Clapham garage and arrested for his part in the murder.

CHAPTER 14

MARY EDWARDS SEEKS FINANCIAL ASSISTANCE IN THE AFTERMATH OF HER SON'S MURDER

Even whilst she was remarried, Mary Edwards would intermittently send, as previously mentioned, 'cadging' (quote) letters to George when he was married with a young family knowing that they were likely to arrive at the rented county police houses both at Bons Farm and at 2, Towneley Cottages, a few days before George was to receive his wages of approximately 90 shillings per week.

Letters from Mrs Edwards, according to archived documents, could request money, but occasionally and unwillingly, George paid bills for his mother and gave her gifts of food and necessities much to the annoyance of Rose which created tensions between her and her husband as expressed briefly in the previous chapter.

George was a very loyal son and supported his mother as much as he was able to do on an occasional basis, but in 1928 shortly after his death, Mary Edwards attempted to maintain this financial help from the County Constabulary and sought this through the representation of a local West Norfolk MP, Major Alan Maclean whose constituency included Downham Market who appealed on her behalf to Lieut. Colonel Sir Vivian Henderson MC MP, undersecretary of State for

Home Affairs to enquire if a grant for Mrs Edwards may be available from the County Police Fund.

A letter from Mr Ronald Wells at the Home Office sent a letter of enquiry to the Chief Constable, Capt. Unett on the 29th April1928 (original letter layout and wording):

Please quote reference number:- Home Office,
495,891/84 Whitehall
SW1

27th. April,1928

Dear Captain Unett,

Many thanks for your letter of the 25th April with regard to Gutteridge's mother: we should be glad to reply to Major McLean as soon as possible.

The question whether a grant could be made from the County Police Fund (under Section 4 (c) of the Police Pensions Act, 1921) depends of course on whether she was wholly or mainly dependent upon her son, but I expect this is the point you have in mind.

Yours sincerely,
(signature)

Ronald Wells

Capt. John Alfred Unett.
Courtesy of the Essex Police Museum Chelmsford

Captain John Alfred Unett (pictured) commissioned Superintendent H. Whiting to personally investigate the matter of Mrs Edward's financial circumstances and the 'cadging' letters of correspondence which still existed at the time.

Rose stated in an interview with Superintendent Whiting that; 'the letters made him [George] angry'. The report by Supt. Whiting further states that these letters caused resentment and rows between PC Gutteridge and his wife Rose and that tensions were exacerbated as Rose was never made privy as to the amount of money unwillingly sent to Mrs Edwards. (Pictured below with George.)

A grainy and very rare photograph of George with his mother Mrs Mary Edwards.
Courtesy, Mr Brian Alexander

However, Rose indicated in the report by Superintendent Whiting that there 'was nothing in the nature of a regular allowance made to his mother'.

ESSEX COUNTY CONSTABULARY 10MAY1928

Telephone No. 15.

DIVISIONAL HEAD QUARTERS,

In reply, please quote
Ref. No.

Braintree.

9th May, 1928.

To The Chief Constable of Essex,

   Mrs Edwards, Downham Market, Norfolk.

   <u>Mother of the late P.C. Gutteridge.</u>

  I beg to report that on the 9th instant I made discreet enquiry of Mrs Gutteridge and she told me, that her husband was born out of wedlock, his mother was subsequently twice married, is now a widow and her age is 59 years.

  Her husband frequently received cadging letters from his mother, usually a few days before the monthly payday and he generally sent her some money, the letters made him angry and caused rows between him and his wife, he did not tell his wife the amount of money he sent, but she gathered from the tone of the replies that he generally sent some money to his mother. As far as I could gather from Mrs Gutteridge these were the only monies sent and there was nothing in the nature of a regular allowance by her husband to his mother.

          H. Whiting

          Superintendent.

Superintendent Whiting compiled his report on the issue to Capt. Unett who replied to Ronald Wells at the Home Office stating that;

Dear Mr Wells

I have caused some enquiries to be made to the extent to which the late PC Gutteridge was in the habit of supporting his mother and enclose herewith copy of a report from my Superintendent on the subject.

Having regard to all the circumstances I hardly think this is a case in which the Police Authority should be called upon to contribute as it would appear from the statement that the contributions were by no means regular nor does it appear that they were made very willingly.

Yours sincerely,
(Capt. Unett's signature)
Chief Constable of Essex

Bill's Personal Effects are Returned to His Widow Rose Gutteridge

This perhaps illustrates one of the saddest aspects of this case and how Rose had to cope with yet another stage of the loss of George by having to collect her husband's effects from Romford Police Station. A very bleak duty in which she had to sign an official and witnessed receipt for three items taken from his body on the day he was murdered. It is quite clear from the jerky and uneven signature, (in comparison with her other flowing examples), that Rose produced for the return of her late husband's effects, that she may have been very distraught, nervous or shaking with grief at the time.

PC 498 Frank Meadows, her brother-in-law witnessed this transaction as can be seen from the document below and no doubt gave her much support at this difficult time. Thankfully, Bill's watch has survived the passing of time and the author had the honour to hold this lovely timepiece courtesy of the Alexander family. It is unclear as to the fate of the electric torch or the scissors Bill was carrying at the time of his murder. Poignantly, these items were returned to Rose the day before her husband's killers went to the gallows – the 31st May 1928.

ESSEX COUNTY CONSTABULARY

COUNTY CONSTABULARY,
QUARTERS, CHELMSFORD.
Reed. – 2 JUN 1928

Romford ____ *Station.* Romford ____ *Division.*

29th May 1928. ____ 19

RECEIVED FROM SUPERINTENDENT ATTRIDGE, of the

ROMFORD POLICE,

   1, Watch.

   1, Electric Torch and

   1, pair of scissors.

being the property of my Late Husband,

P.c. Gutteridge, taken possession of by the Police

on the 27th September 1927.

     Signature. *R. Gutteridge* ....

     Date... *May 30ᵗʰ 1928* ....

     Witness. *G. H. Meadows P.C. 498.*

A copy of the actual receipt Rose had to sign for the return of Bill's effects.

Courtesy of the Essex Police Museum, Chelmsford

170

Bill's Watch by kind permission of Mr Brian Alexander

The First Memorial to PC Gutteridge is Planned and Decided

Following the sad death of Bill Gutteridge, a memorial committee comprising five officers of different ranks within the Essex Constabulary had been set up to consider the options of creating a suitable memorial to the fallen police constable and these were: a stone tablet in the Parish Church of St. Mary the Virgin at Stapleford Abbotts; a suitably engraved gravestone; or a stained glass window in the parish church.

Rose was consulted and was central to the decision-making process and her preference of memorial. It was agreed that a suitably engraved gravestone would be her most popular decision but not, at the request of Rose to be sited at the parish Church of St. Mary the Virgin Stapleford Abbotts, considered by many to be the logical location as Bill, Rose and their children had lived in and had been part of the village community for some time. Rose ruefully explained to the deciding committee that should the decision be made that her husband be interred at St. Mary's, to visit his grave would entail her and her family passing the spot near the two trees on that narrow and inclined section of the Romford to Ongar road where her husband had been murdered, further pointing out that St. Mary's in Stapleford Abbotts Church is also up narrow 'Church Lane' as it remains to this day.

After very careful consideration covering five meetings, the committee honoured Rose's wishes and decided to have a suitably engraved headstone with a kerb surround to the grave paid for by Essex County Constabulary (as Rose was unable to meet the cost of this), where George would be laid to rest at the old Christchurch (Lawns) Cemetery in Cemetery Road (now Lorne Road) at Warley in Brentwood. This offered Rose some consolation in knowing that her husband would be at rest nearby to the home of her very close and supportive eldest sister Agnes (Peg) and her family who lived nearby in Junction Road, Warley. Rose, in her grief must have taken much solace in this arrangement benefitting much from the love and support of Peg often in the coming months and the challenging years to come.

After the funeral, the much-respected and compassionate Bishop of Barking, Dr Inskip was consulted on the wording of the inscription on the memorial, agreeing with Capt. Unett that this should avoid using the word 'murder', erring on the term 'lost his life'. This was agreed by Rose and the County Constabulary Committee.

Throughout this time of decision the Bishop of Barking had taken a central interest in the case of PC Gutteridge and the welfare of his bereaved family this being evident in the letter quoted as below, dated the 6th March 1928 to the Chief Constable Capt. Unett;

From the Bishop of Barking

6th March 1928

'I shall be glad to help in the preparation of the memorial to the late
PC. Gutteridge'. I quite agree with you about not using the word
'murdered' on the memorial stone. How would it be to state that
'he gave his life in the fulfilment of his duty' or to use some kindred
expression'? Much will depend upon what kind of memorial is erected.
Some memorials will only allow a very brief inscription and in any case
brevity may be desirable so far as possible'

Yours sincerely,
J.T. Barking

(Original letter)

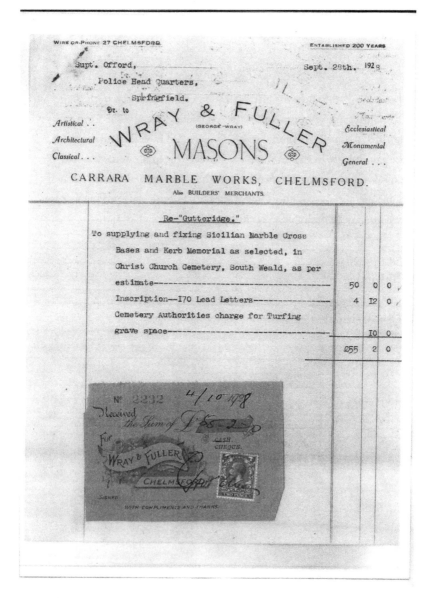

The paid invoice for the grave and photograph of the new and uninscribed Sicilian marble cross sent to Superintendent Offord dated September 28th 1928.

Courtesy of the Essex Police Museum, Chelmsford

The Sicilain marble cross

The firm of Wray and Fuller of Chelmsford were appointed by Essex Constabulary to produce and erect a fine white cross made from Sicilian marble with matching kerb around the grave bearing the inscription in finely placed lead letters:

In proud memory
of
George William Gutteridge,
Police Constable. Essex Constabulary.
Who Met His Death
In The Performance Of Duty
At Stapleford Abbotts
On 27th September 1927
Aged 38
Erected by his comrades

The Grave of PC George Bill Gutteridge at Lorne Road Cemetery, Warley.

Courtesy, of Brian Alexander and the Gutteridge family
Picture by Author

The Grave and Memorial Cross to PC Gutteridge are
Dedicated on the first Anniversary of His Death

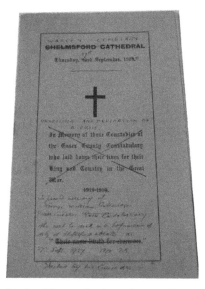

The Original Order of Service for the Dedication of the Memorial to
PC Gutteridge on the first Anniversary of His Death

The Essex Police Museum Chelmsford

The dedication of the memorial by the Bishop of Barking Dr James Insk ip (right of the
picture) with Capt. JA Unett in dress uniform visible also on the right of the picture, on the
first anniversary of the death of PC George William Gutteridge, the 27th September 1928.

Rose, Muriel and her sister Peg are standing to the left of the picture.

Courtesy of the Essex Police Museum, Chelmsford

A close-up picture of the inscription on the Sicilian Marble Cross
marking the last resting place of 'Bill' Gutteridge.

Photo by author

As the years passed and by 1949 as the country and indeed the world, was trying to rebuild itself in the aftermath of another terrible world war, Bill's grave had deteriorated significantly with some of the lead letters becoming detached, cracks appearing on the marble cross and part of the kerbing now having subsided. As mentioned previously, this was a common grave before Bill Gutteridge was interred there and like many ancient and established graves, movement of previously disturbed soil and exposure to the elements (especially rainfall) over a long period of time resulted in this gradual subsidence.

Maintenance of this grave was essentially the responsibility of Essex County Constabulary who no doubt in the war years had to prioritise resources, manpower and funding with grave maintenance falling very much to bottom of the priority scale and Rose of course would not have been strong enough to do this herself.

This important memorial now required specialist attention with the company of A. Pilgrim & Son being appointed to carry out the necessary renovation and repair work and paid for by the Essex County Constabulary, the owners of the headstone and kerbing around the grave.

ESTABLISHED 1882

Telegrams: PILGRIMS, MASONS, ILFORD.
PILGRIMS, MASONS, BRENTWOOD.

Telephones: ILFORD 0838
HAINAULT 2460

Building Masonry
Constructional
and Architectural
———
Old Memorials
Cleaned and Repaired

A. PILGRIM & SON
LEONARD A. PILGRIM
STONE, MARBLE & GRANITE WORKS
155 & 157 GREEN LANE, ILFORD
120 HIGH STREET & KINGS ROAD, BRENTWOOD

Cemetery and
Monumental
Tombs, Headstones,
Crosses.

Designs free on
application.

-8 JUN 1949

The Superintendent of Police,
BRENTWOOD, Essex.

7th June 1949

Re Guttridge Memorial - Christchurch Cemetery
BRENTWOOD

Dear Sir,

Re your call at our Brentwood Office.

We beg to quote to raise Memorial where sunk, for the sum of £2 . 5 . 0.

We beg to quote to thoroughly clean Memorial, by sanding and regritting, scraping between lead letters, stopping up all joints where broken away, Complete for the sum of £10 . 15 . 0.

Trusting to receive your esteemed order, which would have our personal attention.

Yours faithfully,

Leonard. A Pilgrim

pp A. Pilgrim & Son.

Chief Constable of Essex.

The Chairman and Members
of the Administration of Police
Sub-Committee.

The Invoice for raising and renovating the Memorial.

Courtesy, the Essex Police Museum, Chelmsford

Rose and the Children are Given a New Start in Dagenham

Although life was still a big struggle for Rose help was to come; not from the police but from the Derrick family. Ethel May Derrick, the eldest daughter of Mr and Mrs Derrick was also a teacher who then worked at a school in Dagenham.

Ethel had approached London Council and explained the circumstances of Rose's plight following the high-profile murder of her husband George and put Rose in touch with them. Although Rose was not officially eligible as she lived outside of the area, the council authorities cast aside protocol in favour of compassion providing Rose with a second floor flat at 97, Armstead Walk, part of a development in Dagenham to rehouse people from the growing slum clearance of East London where diseases such as tuberculosis were rife due to inadequate sanitation, overcrowded living conditions and poor nutrition.

As will be seen from the letter below that Rose sent to the Chief Constable of Essex advising him of her change of accommodation, an accurate but polite description of the squalid accommodation they had to endure in Albert Road.

Feb. 22nd 1929 97, Armstead Walk
Dagenham
Essex

To : The Chief Constable of Essex

Sir

I beg to inform you, that I have left Braintree having found the two rooms both unsuitable and unhealthy, for the children: for everything had to be done in the one room downstairs including the washing; also the landlady wished for us to leave as soon as we could to let her rooms to men lodgers which she found paid better and which she had already got men lodgers while we were there and I found that the sanitary arrangements were unsuitable for my daughter and myself, having to pass through the room where men were sitting: I am renting a flat at Dagenham with three rooms. Scullery, bathroom etc: the rent which is 12 shillings and sixpence is a lot more than I really can manage to pay but for the children's health I must study: I have tried very hard all round for a house: with a suitable rent but it is very difficult to obtain one, we came last Tuesday week.

We have an upstairs flat of the council houses: I tried hard to get a council house at Braintree but they were very soon occupied.

Yours sincerely, Mrs Gutteridge.

Rose sent the letter advising him of her change of address as payment of her widow's pension would be dependent on making the police authorities aware of any changes in her circumstances. As Muriel Alexander mentioned in an interview with Dr Maureen Scollan in November 1991, the police would make monthly checks on her mother *before* she received her pension to ensure she did not have any men living in the house, had a job or had a male partner as this would have compromised her pension.

Muriel Alexander explained that the policemen assigned to this task seemed to dislike this duty with others being embarrassed to do it with the 'check' being in the form of a 'Hello Mrs Gutteridge' or simply a friendly wave rather than an intrusive questioning of her situation proving that many beat Constables who knew her, still carried out their duties with compassion.

As Muriel went on to say with, I sensed, some resentment in her voice, 'I don't remember anyone from the police coming to see us when we were down there,' (in Braintree).

It just seemed as if they wanted Rose and her children to get out of the police cottage as soon as possible and with minimal welfare or pastoral support and to conclude this sad episode I am reliably informed by a long serving retired police officer, 'That's how things were then' as quoted by Muriel Alexander in a recorded interview with Dr Maureen Scollan, Nov. 1991. At last, due to the combined efforts of Bishop Inskip and the Derrick family; who had monitored the welfare of Rose and the children and with a compassionate listening ear of the housing department at London Council, Rose had been able to rent a relatively modern two bedroom upstairs flat at 97 Armstead Walk, Dagenham. Now it became possible to resume some form of normality with a much healthier and dignified lifestyle for her and her children benefitting from much improved domestic and sanitary amenities at her disposal including a sink and bathroom, washing and bedroom space; the downside being that Rose had to carry her washing downstairs to hang it out on the lines in the garden, collect it and bring it up again and no doubt keeping her fingers crossed that it didn't rain.

Despite her hardship by June 1929 Rose was thinking very much ahead about how Muriel now 14 years old, would cope financially and have some independence, as in two years' time her children's pension of £15. 10s would cease as she reached sixteen. In the meantime Capt. Unett had sent Rose some money, presumably out of police donations which had been held on her behalf but also purchased a savings certificate for Muriel. In a prompt, respectful and eloquent reply Rose wrote to the Chief Constable from her home at 97 Armstead Walk, Dagenham on the 4th June 1929:

To the Chief Constable of Essex

Dear Sir
I gratefully acknowledge, the cheque for £2. 5s received from you this morning, and will you kindly accept my thanks for purchasing the Savings Certificate for the benefit of my Daughter Muriel, who joins with me, for your kind thought.

Yours Gratefully:
Mrs Gutteridge

However, the comparitively improved living conditions Rose and the children now enjoyed came at a price attracting a new weekly rent of 12 shillings and sixpence placing extra pressure on her very limited widow's pension on which she and her children existed. This is very evident in a lamentable letter Rose wrote to the Chief Constable, Capt. Unett, dated November 6th 1929;

Sir,

My wish for seeing you was to ask if you could possibly allow me to have an extra one pound added on to my pension each month, from the money subscribed from the Police forces, as I find that after paying my rent each week which is now 11 shillings and seven pence that I am quite unable to pay the extra out. For the childrens boots, also the doctors bills, of which I now have one in hand, for my little boy who suffers from bronchitis, and who is not at all strong. I would willingly go out to work, but I find that my strength will not allow me to. I trust that you will not think that I am dissatisfied with my pension, as such is not so; but when it comes in getting boots and doctors bills I find it very difficult to manage, I am still looking out for a cottage at a cheaper rent.

Yours truly,
Mrs Gutteridge

The Chief Constable agreed to Rose's request and the £1 was duly taken from the National Savings Certificates held on her behalf but as can be seen from the letter Rose sent to Capt. Unett, Rose did not receive the extra money until the end of June 1930 but the pressure on household expenses increased further in the interim as Rose indicates in the letter of acknowledgement she sent to the Chief Constable dated July 1st 1930.

The letter reads:

July 1st 1930

ESSEX COUNTY CONSTABULARY,
HEADQUARTERS, CHELMSFORD.
Recd. -3 JUL 1930

97 Armstead Walk
Dagenham
S x

To The Chief Constable of Essex

Sir

I beg to acknowledge £1. received this evening of the sale of part of the National Savings Certificates: I will try & see if I can manage to carry on without taking more away from the Savings, as I know I have my two Children to care for, and for their future; its the big rent that makes it very difficult, as it has been raised these last few months again to 12-2 a week; so I will try & leave the remainder & try and manage;

Thanking you Sir

I am Yours Truly:
Mrs N.A.E. Gutteridge

By kind permission and courtesy of, The Essex Police Museum, Chelmsford

185

This further and quite sad letter further illustrates the continual financial struggle Rose endured two years after her husband's death and it is lamentable that if the Bishop of Barking had not encountered some resistance in his efforts to achieve further financial security for Rose and her children, 'begging' letters and the attendant indignity of these appeals Rose had to make to the Chief Constable, her dire circumstances could have been eased.

The load was to be lessened by Muriel, who now at only fourteen years old and astutely aware that in two years' time her children's pension would cease as she reached sixteen placing yet another load on her frail but determined mother, was very determined to help the family survive in a similar way in which her late father assisted his own mother in seeking work to support her.

Going from shop to shop, Muriel managed to convince the owner of a general haberdashery shop in Broad Street in Dagenham that she would be a reliable, honest and keen employee and seeing that she was genuine, they employed her. Now, her compassionate and humanitarian employer being fully aware of the public outrage surrounding the murder of her father and the hardship her mother continually faced, raised her ten shilling weekly wage for very long hours to twelve as Muriel recalled in later years, 'I should have got ten shillings a week but they gave me twelve shillings a week because they felt sorry for me'.

It can be appreciated that, although not a huge sum in those days this extra income, plus the extra consolation of two shillings on top of Muriel's wage did go some way in easing her mother's situation in parallel to the ongoing and active support aunt Agnes gave to Rose in helping clothe Muriel and Jack with suitably altered garments her own children had grown out of.

As Muriel said in later years after all that her mother had been through by this time she had grown weak and unable to work, which was noticed by the ever-vigilant police authorities, who previously offered to have Rose's children Muriel and especially Jack, (with their misguided view that 'boys are harder to bring up') put into the Police School (for orphans). This again proved that they (the police authorities) were watching her but without offering pastoral support and only minimal financial support. Indeed, their letter to Rose coldly stated that the children's allowance to Muriel and Jack awarded to them following their father's death would be used to pay for their keep if they were placed in the Police School.

Rose railed against this using the inner strength she possessed and refused point blank this interference from the authorities, ably demonstrating in her very difficult position that she remained perfectly capable of looking after them herself and no-one was going to take her children away, quoted by Muriel Alexander as saying, 'No, they're as dear to me as each other'.[2]

---

2 **Footnote:** Author's view: The style, expression and choice of words
   Rose uses in all her written correspondence given the hardship and
   trials she faced after George's death is dignified, always polite, clear and
   unambiguous; devoid of any level of high emotion, aggression, threat or
   otherwise. Having read the original letters Rose composed, it became clear
   that she had an unshakeable love of her family and their welfare, never
   referring to her own difficulties even after suffering the further loss of
   her close sister Minnie May Irene five years later in 1932 at the early age
   of 44 years and leaving her brother-in-law George Meadows a widower.
   Minnie is buried at the cemetery in Braintree (pictured).

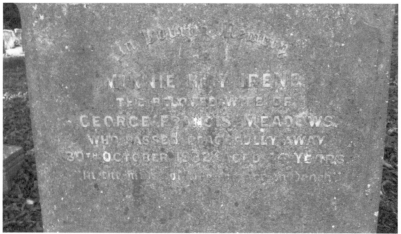

Pictures courtesy of Braintree Cemetery

CHAPTER 15

JOHN AND MURIEL MEET AGAIN

As time passed and with a further move to a very much more suitable house for Rose and her children at 53, Ford Road Dagenham, Muriel had the chance to advance herself into dressmaking but her new employer was in London. She travelled there and back each day from Dagenham but the hand of fate was to take over as John, still living at Stapleford Abbotts at the home of his parents, Harry and Ethel Alexander at 3 Towneley Cottages, had secured a job at Fords of Dagenham.

Over time, John had made many friends within the large department where he worked at Fords and somehow found out in conversation with them that Rose, Muriel and Jack were living close by in Dagenham and his heart must have leapt at this news.

This reunion was meant to be with John finding out where the childhood sweetheart he missed so much, lived. With some trepidation and probably a lot of nerves, John called at the house. Rose answered and was probably extremely surprised but pleased to see John and lost no time in telling him that if he went to Dagenham station at a certain time he could meet Muriel as she got off the train which he did, their childhood romance rekindling very quickly.

The year was 1936 and John knew in his heart that this chance discovery was meant to be and Muriel would be the only one for him, their time apart evaporating quickly. John wasted no time in composing a letter to Rose asking politely in the gentlemanly way of his character and that of his upbringing, if he could marry Muriel.

Rose was a very astute, level-headed lady with a great insight into how the strong relationship between Muriel and John, witnessed from a distance, had started to blossom in those early days as they gazed fondly over the garden fence at each other in the happier days before Bill's death and probably in her heart knew, and hoped, that fate would eventually reunite them. Rose considered John's traditional and polite request and in a letter dated the 21st May 1936, Rose replied to John;

Dear John,
In reply to your letter asking consent of you being engaged to Muriel.

I have no objection so long as you both have considered the matter over carefully and quite understand you love each other sufficiently to always be happy together and to share your two lives for each other. You already know what a sweet disposition Muriel has so I sincerely trust you will look after her for me, but I do not think I need worry of you having her, and to do your duty to love and take care of her always; for I know she will look after you, and love and care only for you; and that is what it should be, for both of you.

Kind regards
From Mrs Gutteridge

John and Muriel were married in Dagenham on the 26th October 1938 as the build up to the Second World War Intensified.

In the years following Bill's death, Rose spoke very little about the murder of her husband and it was rarely discussed. The children were even advised to keep their distance from other children at school who bore the surnames of Browne or Kennedy or similar, should they possibly be related in some way to the families of the murderers who had been hanged in May 1928 and may try to seek misguided retribution. Brian Alexander informed me that it wasn't until he was 17 (he was born in 1944), that he surprisingly learnt about his grandfather's murder. 'It was never spoken about,' he said, such was the enduring pain and grief the family still held.

There were regular attempts by the Essex Constabulary to recruit Brian, now a tall man with a big presence in the mould of his grandfather, into the Essex County Constabulary when he came of age. But when these occasional visits were made by senior policemen to the family home in Dagenham for this purpose, his mother Muriel became very uneasy and sometimes tearful; fearful that history was in danger of repeating itself and Brian, aware by now of how his late and much respected grandmother Rose who had passed away in 1956 and to whom he had become very close as a child, may have felt and reacted, always declined these regular offers thus illustrating clearly the respect he held for his mother, late grandmother and the grandfather he had lost so tragically in 1927.

In the years following, John Alfred 'Jack' Gutteridge, Bill's son, became a Special Constable in the Dagenham area for a time, shown in a striking photograph in the Gutteridge family archives as seen below.

Special Constable 462 Jack Gutteridge.

by kind permission of Mr Stephen and Mr Christopher Gutteridge

Rose Gutteridge is Finally Reunited with Her Husband George

Rose Gutteridge in later years, seated third from left, approximately a year before she passed away.

By kind Courtesy of Brian Alexander

Rose Gutteridge had soldiered on bravely with happiness in her quiet dignity with her family at the centre of her life as always, but she had been unwell for some time. One could speculate that the enormous worry, stresses and strains she suffered 29 years earlier when she lost her young 38-year-old husband of 14 years in the prime of his life, in such tragic circumstances must have had a marked effect upon her health; the trial of identifying her husband at the mortuary, the very large and public funeral, the invasive press 'jackals', the inquest and subsequent trial at the Old Bailey in April 1928 where she was in the presence of her husband's killers, both at which she was called to give evidence bravely doing so in an almost state of collapse, to say nothing of the continual hardship she endured in the years following.

This terrible journey from happiness and security in a country village to unimaginable grief and hardship really does portray the innate and exceptional strength Rose possessed in sacrificing, at times, her own wellbeing, in favour of the nuclear family of her fiercely loved children in the absence of the man she had lost and, for Rose was irreplaceable. But as Rose entered her twilight years there was, as is normal in a close and loving family, something of a 'role reversal' and now it was a natural progression for Muriel and Jack to return the care to their mother as she had shown them as children and young adults, doing so with the same care and devotion as they had enjoyed.

As her health continued to deteriorate she was taken to St. George's Hospital in Hornchurch near to where Jack and his wife Eva lived in Lyndhurst Drive, but sadly on Saturday the 18th February 1956 at 69 years old, Rose passed away. Note: The death certificate states that Rose was 69 although other official documents place her age at 71 years. (She was born in 1886.)

St.George's Hospital Sutton's Lane, Hornchurch.
Courtesy of the Romford Recorder, Archant Ltd

Very aware of the wishes of Rose, and the family's desire that she would be laid to rest with George in the previously checked grave, Jack ensured that these wishes were passed on to the relevant authorities and by 12.45pm the same day a message had reached Romford Police Station by Bennett's Undertakers in Warley, Brentwood who had been advised earlier of Rose's death in preparation for her funeral. It Read:

Sir, I beg to report that at 12.45pm Saturday, the 18th February, 1956, a telephone message was received at this station from Mr Lowe, Graves Superintendent of Brentwood (Telephone number BRENTWOOD 741) to the effect that Mr Gutteridge of Lyndhurst Drive, Hornchurch, desires the body of his mother (who died in St. George's Hospital, Hornchurch last night) the wife of ex PC Gutteridge, to be buried in the same grave as her late husband.

Ex. PC Gutteridge is buried in a common grave – number B.131 – at the Old Christchurch Cemetery, Lorne Road, Warley Hill, Brentwood – thus we have no rights in the matter, but did provide the tombstone, which will be removed and replaced with care. The undertakers dealing will be Bennett's of Brentwood. Mr Lowe informs us of this as a matter of courtesy.

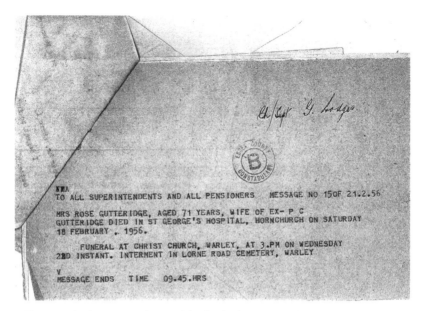

The internal police memo advising of the death of Rose Gutteridge and that the funeral would be held at Christchurch followed by confirmation that Rose would be interred in Lorne Road cemetery at 3pm on the 28ᵗʰ February 1956.

Essex Police Museum

A much more private family funeral, again conducted very sympathetically by Bennett's Undertakers of Brentwood ensured that Rose would quietly take her last journey to join George in Lorne Road Cemetery which she did on Wednesday 28ᵗʰ February 1956 this time devoid of the massive outpouring of public grief, crowds of onlookers and supporters, the huge police presence and the media she had to bravely endure on Saturday the 1ˢᵗ October 1927 when prematurely saying her goodbyes to George at what was to be in years hence, their joint resting place.

Rest in Peace Rose.

Jack, as many men did in this heavily industrialised area of Essex, had chosen to work at Fords of Dagenham, the biggest employer in the area, becoming a successful toolmaker. Jack, I am informed, was also a very talented amateur photographer, his family benefitting greatly from this skill. Jack was 24 years old when he met Eva, his wife-to-be and they had two sons together, Stephen and Christopher but sadly, Jack died suddenly on Good Friday the 28th March 1986 (predeceasing his elder sister Muriel) at the age of 62. This time, the firm of T. Cribb and Son, Funeral Directors in Hornchurch conducted he funeral arrangements and he was cremated and in a moving family gathering, his ashes were later scattered on Lawn 37 in area 10 of the beautifully landscaped and peaceful area of the South Essex Crematorium at Marks Tey near Upminster.

Sadly, Jack Passed away before seeing the roadside memorial to his late father established in 1990 four years after his death.

John and Muriel steadfastly remained in Dagenham for the rest of their lives, John working at Fords until he retired and together, he and Muriel seeing the hub of the family grow as grandchildren and great grandchildren came along but in May 1996 Muriel passed away at the wonderful age of 80 years. She was cremated and her ashes placed in a separate memorial within the kerbing in Grave B131 at Lorne Road Cemetery appropriately rejoining her parents George and Rose. John followed Muriel 10 years later in October 2006 having achieved a wonderful 92 years. He was cremated and of course joined the love of his life Muriel, in their own memorial in Grave B131.

At last, a family reunited.

The memorial to Muriel and John Alexander sadly discoloured and awaiting restoration.

Picture by author

CHAPTER 16

A ROADSIDE MEMORIAL IS RAISED TO THE MEMORY OF PC GEORGE WILLIAM GUTTERIDGE

A chance conversation set in motion an initiative which would prove to be the the most visible and prominent memorial to PC Gutteridge set almost in the form of a gravestone on the main Romford to Ongar road close to where Bill was murdered.

A relative of the late John Alfred 'Jack' Gutteridge was holidaying at her caravan in Clacton when by chance, she got into conversation with a passing young beat policeman. The subject of Bill Gutteridge arose with the young PC listening intently to the whole tale of his brutal murder and probably due to his age, was unaware of this sad event. Somehow, this story reached the attention of Chief Constable Mr John Burrow, a strong supporter in the case of Bill Gutteridge and of policemen who fell in the line of duty, who instigated a proposal to erect a suitable and fitting roadside memorial close to where Bill Gutteridge fell as he did not wish Bill's memory to fall into obscurity on that now much altered and very busy B175 Romford to Ongar road.

A fundraising initiative was launched and the inscribed granite stone was paid for by Epping and Ongar police officers, supported further by grants from Epping Forest Council, Stapleford Abbotts and Lambourne Parish Councils. The memorial was raised in 1990, also the 150th Anniversary of Essex Police; a very appropriate date and chosen by local police officers. This important memorial was officially and ceremonially unveiled by Muriel Alexander (nee-Gutteridge) and Mr John Burrow, the Chief Constable of Essex who said at the unveiling, 'We remember an officer who served this community; an officer who, in the best traditions of the Essex Police, gave his life in the course of his duty. This stone will be reminder to local people, to local officers, of the sacrifice of that officer.'

After the unveiling, Muriel Alexander, then 74 years of age said 'I think it is a lovely gesture. I think it is very very good of them to still remember my dad.' She went to say, 'I know it's a long time ago but it is still fresh in my mind. It's something you can never forget.'

Standing proudly at the northern end of Gutteridge Lane with the beautiful Rose Cottage in the background, a bronze plaque on granite states to the passer-by and those who have stopped (some out of curiosity) to pay their respects. It reads:

Close By This Spot
PC George William Gutteridge
Was Murdered 27th September 1927

The late Muriel Alexander at the unveiling of the roadside memorial in 1990 by the Chief Constable of Essex Constabulary, Mr John Burrow (with back to camera).

Courtesy of Mr Brian Alexander

The Proud Roadside Memorial to PC George William Gutteridge at How Green,
Stapleford Abbotts

For many years and before the B175 Romford to Ongar road had
been reprofiled to accommodate increasing volumes of road traffic, a
small wooden sign had existed to mark the spot where Bill Gutteridge
was murdered and was thought to be lost over the intervening years
possibly during road construction work. Thankfully this complete
but yellowing cardboard memorial (previous location unknown) was
rescued and taken as a mark of respect to Bill Gutteridge, to the Essex
Police Museum where it is on display to this day. (See below.)

Courtesy of the Essex Police Museum, Chelmsford

A Bronze Memorial is Raised to the Memory of PC 'Bill' Gutteridge in St. Mary the Virgin, Parish Church of Stapleford Abbotts

One of the author's first meetings with the eldest grandson of Bill Gutteridge and his wife Valerie took place at the Parish Church of Stapleford Abbotts on a bright and blustery 14th May 2015 during one of the popular flower festivals provided by this wonderful close-knit church community who cherish their church with an enviable fervour; proudly welcoming those who have wound their way up the very narrow Church Lane to be greeted quietly, but enthusiastically by the church community who work so hard to provide and celebrate the many family-orientated activities which occur throughout the seasons, seamlessly linked to the ecclesiastical calendar in a very 'English' way.

Brian Alexander was keen to show me aspects of the church including permanent memorials to those lost and wounded in the First and Second World Wars (including his other grandad Harry Alexander the postman who was wounded by rifle fire in the Great War). My eyes fell upon a beautiful watercolour painting depicting the church itself (pictured).

St. Mary the Virgin, Parish Church of Stapleford Abbotts
by the talented artist John Alexander.

Photo courtesy of Brian Alexander

203

Brian could see that I admired this greatly and wishing to know who the artist was, Brian said, 'My father, John Alexander painted that,' indicating that he had produced several more, pointing to those displayed on the opposite wall and placed there for all to see during harvest festival but which are stored safely in the parish archives.

I commented on the beauty of these paintings of the local community as I cannot hide my enthusiasm for innate talent which his late father undoubtedly possessed. As we both took in the spirit of the occasion including the wonderful tea and cakes provided by the ladies of the church, I nostalgically wandered around this small church almost searching for a memorial to Bill Gutteridge but this was nowhere to be seen. 'Is there a memorial to your granddad in the church Brian?' I enquired. He quietly replied out of earshot of others who may have taken offence, 'No, but there should be.'

As was mentioned previously in this work, in 1928 his widowed grandmother Rose had the choice offered to her by the appointed police memorial committee to have a suitably engraved gravestone in the churchyard or alternatively, a stone tablet or a stained glass window in George's memory to be raised within the church of St. Mary's but as we now understandably realise, it would have meant that she would have had to pass the spot where her husband had been murdered. Her choice was to have her husband laid to rest at Lorne Road Cemetery with a suitably engraved gravestone where she could also be close to her sister Agnes who lived nearby in Junction Road. At this point I put it to Brian that with his permission, I would be prepared to lead an initiative to have a memorial plaque installed in the church of St. Mary the Virgin to his grandfather's memory; after all, this was the parish church of the village he was patrolling and protecting on the morning of his murder.

Never one to mince words, Brian readily agreed to my proposal as he astutely recognised that I was deadly serious about this. I said that I would 'put the wheels in motion' beginning with a letter of proposal to the vicar, The Rev. Canon Roger Gayler, a very forward-thinking man who enthusiastically welcomed this initiative. Not having dealt with church authorities in the past (this was new territory for me), I composed a letter with the permission of Brian Alexander proposing that a suitable bronze memorial to his Grandfather, the late PC Gutteridge be raised to a suitable and agreed position in St. Mary's Church; a central and prominent part of the community Bill Gutteridge was responsible for, up until his untimely death.

The letter of proposal was presented at the next meeting of the Parochial Church Council and was unanimously agreed in principle. At a subsequent meeting the PCC further discussed and identified a prominent place in the church where the plaque could be sited, the dimensions, wording and background colour. Following a large number of e-mails, letters and discussions to say nothing of multiple draft images compiled digitally by the foundry appointed to manufacture the plaque, the strict criteria laid down by the diocese was finally met and an official 'Faculty' (planning and request) document was compiled by the church and sent to the Diocese of Chelmsford for the consideration of the Diocesan Court.

Months passed, (I have been reliably informed that church matters such as this move at a snails pace!), then after more months had passed, I received news from the administration department at St. Mary's that the Chelmsford Diocesan Court had approved the proposal and that we could proceed with no objections being raised. Much heartened, I could now instruct Anglia Casting Ltd. of Horsford, a specialist memorial foundry near Norwich (very appropriate as Bill Gutteridge was Norfolk born and bred), to manufacture the plaque first providing them with a copy of the approved faculty document. They not only gave their immediate attention to this but provided an electronic photographic record of the casting process. The result was stunning, being beautifully presented with the raised and polished inscription and of course, it was very heavy! Very appropriately, this was carefully sent by carrier to the home of Brian Alexander who would then present it to the church for their approval and in the meantime a suitable light oak mount was sourced in preparation to carry the memorial.

By kind permission and direction of the vicar, the author and Brian Alexander attached the bronze memorial to the north wall of the church with great care and precision using some very long brass screws to ensure that it remained in place for many years to come. To enrich this further Brian attached a head and shoulders photograph of his helmeted grandfather in uniform so that the visitor may be able to relate more closely to the lovely bronze memorial. Since the unveiling, a long-serving member of the church has framed the photograph in a similar light oak to that of the memorial mount.

The Bronze Memorial Plaque to Bill Gutteridge proudly adorns the north wall of St. Mary the Virgin, Stapleford Abbotts raised by subscription from the Gutteridge and Alexander families and the local community including the village school

After the unveiling, pictured left to right: Bernard Mullin, (author), Inspector Martyn Lockwood, (author and authority on the murder of PC Gutteridge), Chief Superintendent and Commander of the Western Division, Essex Police, Mr Sean 'O Callaghan, Mr Brian Alexander, the first grandson of PC Gutteridge

The unveiling date was set at the suggestion of the vicar and to form part of the church harvest festival celebrations. Very appropriately, this was to be the 24th September 2016 and by happy unplanned coincidence would have been the wedding anniversary of George and Rose; they were married on the 24th September 1913 at Fordham Church 103 years previously. The vicar and the Parochial Church Council of Fordham Church very kindly provided a full size Union Jack flag used on special and national occasions, as did Norfolk Constabulary by supplying an emblazoned and beautiful silk drape standard with the crest of Norfolk Constabulary standing proud by kind permission of the Chief Constable to jointly adorn the new memorial. The beautifully crested Essex Police silk drape standard appropriately took centre position below the new bronze memorial claiming PC George William Gutteridge 'as one of their own' but also marking the constant affiliation of Norfolk and Essex Constabularies. These precious and rare standards were respectfully raised to their respective positions prior to the ceremony by members of the church community including the author's sister Mrs Bernadette Dudney whose keen eye ensured the accuracy, attachment and position of the standards.

The ceremony was honoured to have the presence of Police Inspector Martyn Lockwood of Essex Police, author and authority on the murder of PC Gutteridge who very kindly unveiled the Union Jack-draped new memorial in the presence of Stephen and Christopher Gutteridge and Brian Alexander (Bill's grandsons) accompanied in this exceptionally cohesive and special event with a rare gathering of several generations of the Gutteridge and Alexander families, the supportive community of Stapleford Abbotts and representatives of The National Association of Retired Police Officers (NARPO) together with The National Police Officers Roll of Honour local representative for Essex plus a host of other guests.

Prior to the unveiling the vicar, The Reverend Canon Roger Gayler read a tribute to PC George Gutteridge composed by His Grace the Very Reverend Peter Hill, the current Area Bishop of Barking, followed by prayers and much lively discussion at this important commemorative event.

Retracing Bill's Last Walk With his First Grandson Brian Alexander

Over the last 90 years there has been some speculation and discussion regarding the spot where Bill Gutteridge was *actually* murdered although his roadside memorial, erected and dedicated in 1990 states that 'Close to this spot, PC George William Gutteridge was Murdered on the 27th September 1927', a short distance uphill from where Bill actually fell. This wonderful and steadfast memorial stands proudly at How Green almost in front of Rose Cottage for all those passing or wishing to stop to pay their respects and realistically, it remains on this very busy section of road, not the most accurate, but the safest point to appreciate the ultimate sacrifice Bill Gutteridge made in upholding law and order in the village he took under his wing and fiercely protected.

To position the memorial 638 yards down from Grove House at the most approximate position (within yards) would have prevented many from paying homage to Bill as there is no pavement to stroll along or a small layby, as the roadside memorial is fortunate to have, to pull in off the very busy road and to stop. The evidence given by those at the trial of Browne and Kennedy in April 1928 states that the fatal shooting took place 638 yards south of Grove House atop How Green Hill (the conference point), where Bill met PC Sydney Taylor before proceeding down the road toward Pinchback Bridge and further on to his police cottage in Tysea Hill both of which he never reached. This distance was stated at the trial of Browne and Kennedy, Notable British Trials, W. Teignmouth Shore, 1930, (William Hodge and Company, Edinburgh and Glasgow), by the Constable PC Frederick Masters assigned to take measurements and to accurately plot the area in which the murder took place. Examined by Mr Roome, he stated to the court that;

'I am a Police Constable and am accustomed to preparing plans. I prepared Exhibit No.46, which is a plan showing a portion of the road between Romford and Ongar. I was shown a spot on the road marked in the lower as the spot where the body was found. It is not so marked on the plan, but it is section of that plan where the width is written as 17ft. 6'. From that spot to the conference point at Grove House is a distance of 638 yards...'

Discussions with others most notably Mr Brian Alexander seemed to indicate that the spot where his grandfather fell was now a little unclear due to the series of road improvements and reprofiling which had taken place over many years thereby 'blurring' the actual spot the terrible act, as regarded in many quarters as the crime of the century, had occurred but the left side of the B175 on which Grove House stands is still quite straight making the measurement of the approximate distance somewhat easier.

As always, Brian Alexander remained positive and keen to ensure geographical accuracy for the sake of his grandfather's memory. The walk we subsequently took together will remain with me for the rest of my life. This surreal experience of walking beside the first grandson of PC George Gutteridge as we traced as accurately as possible the last steps of the final and tragic journey his grandfather took that early and misty morning of Tuesday the 27th of September 1927 never reaching home or completing his shift was somehow an honour to perform in representation of my mother and grandparents who Bill Gutteridge was essentially protecting at the time of his death.

Led by Brian Alexander, this once in a lifetime experience began opposite the gates of the magnificent Grove House where Bill had stood before his fateful walk home and from where we started walking down toward Pinchback Bridge following the old section of the road past Rose Cottage in How Green at which the initial alarm was raised.

This old section of the road has now been renamed 'Gutteridge Lane' thanks to the dedicated efforts of Mrs Sally Rogers whose beautiful cottage has been her and her husband Bryan's home for many years and where Alec Ward ran to and alerted Alfred Perritt of his terrible discovery, together briskly walking 250 yards downhill to where the body of Bill Gutteridge lay.

Brian Alexander and I walked past Rose Cottage and past the left fork in the road looking down the long quiet lane leading towards Mitchell's Farm, the former residence of Mr Montague 'Monty' Martin who, among others had reported hearing shots in the early hours of Tuesday 27th September 1927 and believing it to be poachers, went back to sleep.

The crescent shaped Gutteridge Lane now abruptly ended at the southern end, the old road presenting itself as a bank where we had to turn right to exit back onto the busy B175 road and continue our walk. But faced with this 'bank' we took time to stop and visualise the course of the old road as it may have been. As a child at my grandparents' bungalow home nearby and long since demolished as have most of the old properties in the same location, I remembered the road as it used to be although the passage of time has blurred my memory a little, but Brian, with the benefit of a few years my senior and of course a far sharper knowledge, memory and appreciation of this part of Stapleford Abbotts imparted to him by his parents Muriel and John, Harry and Ethel Alexander, and most importantly his grandmother Rose.

We were now into the realms of approximation and for a very small part, speculation. As we crossed the busy road adorned with high visibility jackets I wondered for a moment what Bill Gutteridge would have had to say about how his beat had altered? We reached the far side where High House Farm still stood and the almost original pathway, hidden by an avenue of trees which ran its original course south towards Pinchback Bridge.

Still feeling honoured to be accompanying the first grandson of PC Gutteridge on this fact finding journey, we continued to walk until the measuring wheel had recorded the 638 yard point, parallel with the opposite side of the road where the murder took place now adorned with established trees and of course reasonably close to the wonderful roadside memorial a little further up the road for all to see, reflect on and remember the ultimate sacrifice of a brave village policeman; PC George William Gutteridge, 1889–1927.

CHAPTER 17

A COMMUNITY REMEMBERS ONE OF THEIR OWN; PC GEORGE WILLIAM 'BILL' GUTTERIDGE

It is appropriate that the two examples represented below of members of the community of Stapleford Abbotts are recognised here (with their permission) highlighting their attempts and achievements in maintaining the memory of PC George William Gutteridge. There are many others in the village, most notably archivists and members of the Historical Society, church members of the Parish Church of Stapleford Abbotts, St. Mary the Virgin, along with those in the wider community who have pursued an individual interest in maintaining the memory of their village policeman in their own precise and dedicated way.

Sally's Personal Crusade To Establish Gutteridge Lane

As is well known, Rose Cottage was the first port of call by Alec Ward to raise the alarm to Alfred Perritt, an insurance agent; a short time later alerting the authorities by telephone having driven to Stapleford Tawney Post Office to announce the grim discovery he had made on that fateful September morning.

Set as now, just off the main Ongar to Brentwood road a 'chocolate box' 14th century cottage of stunning beauty partly occupying crown land, Rose Cottage suddenly became an historical landmark in this terrible murder and what could be described as the startpoint of the huge manhunt for the killers of PC Gutteridge, which was to ensue.

In later years it was decided by Essex Highways Department to re-profile a long stretch of the B175 and effectively by-pass Rose Cottage which I am told by the current long term residents Sally and Bryan Rogers that Rose Cottage benefitted from the redirection of a growing volume of traffic i.e less traffic vibration to this ancient building and a quieter environment for the occupants. Thankfully however, the old section of road was retained as an access road to Rose Cottage, Mitchell's farm and other properties in the area to what was known locally as How Green with the splendid Grove House standing prominently on the brow of How Green Hill overlooking the gentle incline of the Romford to Ongar road.

Sally and Bryan Rogers have lovingly maintained Rose Cottage over the past 45 years becoming famous in the past for serving very popular cream teas during the summer months to people, some who had travelled long distances, to sit in the lovely gardens of Rose Cottage.

But Sally very astutely sensing that the memory of Bill Gutteridge was in danger of gradually being eroded, went a step further in sending a letter of proposal to Epping Forest District Council that this almost crescent shaped section of the old road be renamed 'Gutteridge Way' in enduring dedication and remembrance to the Late PC George Gutteridge. Dated the 30th December 1990 it read:

Dear Sirs,
The police have recently erected a memorial to PC Gutteridge, who was killed in the execution of duty outside Rose Cottage in 1927.

Since the lane in which we are situated is unnamed (it used to be part of Stapleford Road), we think it would be a nice gesture, to call the lane 'Gutteridge Way', in honour of the Police Constable who gave his life on behalf of our community.

We await your comments with interest,

Yours sincerely,
Sally Rogers

This was respectfully considered by Epping Forest District Council who gave this proposal their early consideration and in a letter of reply to Sally Rogers dated 21st January 1991, Mr Keith Sharman, District Engineer and Surveyor wrote:

Dear Mrs Rogers,

Further to my Council's letter of 10th January on the possibility of naming the lane at How Green I am in the process of undertaking consultation with the various organisations, eg Post Office, Police and the Parish Council, on your suggestion. I intend, if possible, that the matter be discussed at the appropriate committee meeting at the end of February.

With regard to the name it does seem to me that Gutteridge Lane would be more appropriate in a rural setting to Gutteridge Way and I have

suggested this to the consultees as an alternative. Please let me know if this would be acceptable to you.

Yours sincerely, K. Sharman, District Engineer and Surveyor

It can be imagined that Sally was very encouraged by this letter and that her proposal had been given serious and prompt consideration. Sally responded with a buoyant letter to Keith Sharman:

Thank you for your letter of 21st. January 1991.

We confirm that your suggestion of Lane as an alternative to Way is quite acceptable, the emphasis is, of course, on 'Gutteridge' for reasons explained. Thank you for keeing us informed.

Yours sincerely.

This significant proposal by Sally Rogers was fully agreed and the section of road was duly named 'Gutteridge Lane', being prominently signposted 'Gutteridge Lane' at both ends preserving for all generations to come a valuable section of the 'old' Romford to Ongar Road with which those with an interest in PC Gutteridge could visualise and identify with and how the road may have looked in the late 1920s.

Signed for the visitor and community at both ends of the lane.
Photo by Author

Bob's personal tribute to PC George William 'Bill' Gutteridge

The Late Bob Coon 10.08.1937–12. 10.2007.

By kind permission of Mrs, Elizabeth Coon

Bob Coon (pictured above) spent most of his life in Stapleford Tawney and latterly lived at Stapleford Abbotts with his Wife Elizabeth at 2, Towneley Cottages (the former home of Bill and Rose Gutteridge and their children) until his sudden death in 2007.

Bob worked, apart from completing three years of national service in the RAF, with horses for the old and established firm of T. Cribb and Son in Murthering Lane off Tysea Hill. This famous and highly respected family firm really set the benchmark for quality in supplying horses for funerals and major events and it was in the notable Highgate Cemetery in North London (the burial place of Karl Marx, Michael Faraday and many other famous names), where Bob, who was working there tending his horses at a funeral, collected some pine seeds to take back to Stapleford Abbotts with him and 'Bob being Bob' had a preconceived idea for their use.

The roadside memorial near Rose Cottage had been established and duly dedicated in 1990 by the Chief Constable Mr John Burrow in the presence of the late Muriel Alexander who, with the Chief Constable jointly unveiled the memorial. Bob wished to show respect for Bill Gutteridge, in his own way by planting three of his pine seeds near to the memorial of the much respected village policeman whose cottage he now owned and occupied with his family.

Bob nurtured and cared for this sapling as it grew from the seed he had planted nearby but sadly as this sapling began to grow in earnest, it was stolen by someone who may have taken it for personal gain or as an act of vandalism probably unaware of its significance.

Mrs Coon explained to me that it really upset her late husband and others in the community who were aware of Bob's personal dedication to the memory of Bill Gutteridge, very disappointed by this selfish theft.

They characteristically acted upon it immediately, replacing the stolen sapling with a new thriving young tree which stands behind the memorial and well rooted to this day.

As we recall, Bob had brought several pine seeds back from Highgate Cemetery and undeterred, planted another at his place of work where it has flourished and remains as Bob's dedication to Bill.

Bob was so greatly respected by T. Cribb and Son that a memorial to him was raised by his colleagues and employer existent today in the stables where he worked and knew so well before his sudden death.

Photo by kind permission of Mr Peter Gibson, T. Cribb and Son, Murthering Lane Stapleford Abbotts

The Murder of PC Gutteridge and Tales of the Supernatural

There is belief in some quarters that a life taken too soon may leave an 'imprint' upon the environment it occupied in life and that the spirit in its quest for peace and to pass over may, as some believe revisit or return to retrace their steps, searching for a reason for their early demise perhaps, or to complete a duty, journey or task, never completed in life.

The 'Top Oak' was regularly frequented by Bill Gutteridge during his life in Stapleford Abbotts as was the Rabbits pub at the other end of the village in former years before the refurbishment of the Oak and the development of new housing covering the position where the old coach house once stood, where Bill's body lay under guard overnight before he was taken to the mortuary at Oldchurch Hospital for post-mortem examination the following day.

The long serving established and level headed mature-minded staff have occasionally reported having seen a caped figure brush past them in the dim late hours when customers had departed as they were tidying up.

Not easily frightened, they also reported feeling no fear in their experience, just surprise and questioning.

Others have reported the sound of heavy footfall made by the sound of boots along the old part of the road between Grove House at How Green down through Gutteridge Lane past Rose Cottage and on toward Pinchback Bridge and ultimately to Towneley Cottages in Tysea Hill, in the twilight hours. Some have said that Bill is trying to complete his beat and return home; his spirit imprisoned in time and yearning for rest.

Another account is similarly interesting but even more so as the person who had this experience was, at the time, completely unware of the murder of PC George Gutteridge.

The account is as follows;

'When I was a child I loved to hear ghost stories and I used to ask family members, particularly the older members, whether they had ever seen a ghost.

My father told me that when he was a young man, he was driving through Epping Forest on his way to visit his grandparents in rural essex, when he saw a uniformed policeman standing in the middle of the road, with one hand raised, signalling him to stop. It was late in December, and it was already dark on this isolated and lonely road.

Apprehensively, my father stopped his car, turned to roll down the window, stuck his head out, and began to ask, 'Is there a problem Constable?' When he looked up the policeman was nowhere to be seen. To his amazement, he had completely disappeared, as though he had just evaporated into the surrounding woods!

Puzzled still, my father continued with his journey and on arrival told his grandparents of his experience, wondering whether he could just have imagined it? His grandfather quietly listened, asked where he had seen the policeman and then straight away told him that it was not just his imagination, what he had seen was the ghost of PC George Gutteridge, who had been murdered on that particular stretch of road in Epping Forest. My father had been unaware of this, as the murder had taken place back in 1927. His grandparents were very familiar with the case and they had also heard rumours that his ghost could still be seen on occasion to that day.'

Courtesy of Hawkeyes 1. Do you Have a Ghost Story?

Having conducted some general research on why the presence of those who died suddenly and prematurely as in the case of Bill Gutteridge *might* have remained on the earthly plane, I have found that a wide range of beliefs within these articles share a range of common factors, theories and speculation, examples of which are given below.

There is a belief in some quarters that the spirit or presence of the suddenly deceased may remain for a time in the community or area they frequented where they lost their lives, sudden death having removed them from the normal time continuum as we know it, this effectively standing still at the point of their demise and leaving them in a timeless, dreamlike void before acceptance allows them to pass over.

Another features the view that the suddenly deceased simply *do not know or accept* that they are dead and are confused in not being able to communicate with people they knew in life; possibly feeling guilty in having left their loved ones too soon and possibly uncared for, remaining on another plane to watch over their family; Rose and the children?

The paranormal is an extremely wide and potentially emotive field of study, subject to individual beliefs, radical and sensationalist views and reports, culture and religious orientation, but it is for the reader to arrive at their own conclusion regarding paranormal beliefs.

For me, I keep an open mind.

Reflecting on the life and Murder of PC George William 'Bill' Gutteridge

The murder of Bill Gutteridge has often been referred to as a 'sad case' and this has much foundation if one looks back over the life of this brave policeman suddenly, unexpectedly and very needlessly taken from his family and community in the prime of life leaving a bitterly grieving widow with two young children. The act of his murder was gratuitous and unquestioningly brutal, but in a wider sense this brutality had a major 'ripple' effect in the way it affected the lives of many others, most importantly the quiet Essex community of Stapleford Abbotts. Looking back at the portrait of his life we can see beyond the police uniform which shows the true unwavering spirit, determination and loyalty of a man born into hard Norfolk village life without a guiding father figure and of his own volition chose to start work at eight years old to support his twice married and continually dependant mother.

Forsaking school at times to be the breadwinner, which would hold him back academically when he tried to improve life for himself and his young family by entering (and failing) his sergeants' exams in later years which would have enhanced his income, he did not give up.

He had pursued the girl he had fallen in love with by enlisting with the Essex County Constabulary to be near Rose or 'Annettie' as he called her but in the process, had sacrificed his own 'comfort zone' of a country existence of which he was familiar and its pace of life, to a world of continual strife, violence and criminal activity in the Thames Estuary towns which challenged him in many ways in the tense years leading up to and post Word War 1.

During the war he served his country on home ground training new recruits in addition to completing his own training as a gunner.

After the war, he enthusiastically and with much foresight, took the opportunity to take his new wife Rose and little daughter Muriel away from this uncomfortable urban existence by applying for a country posting taking them back to where their hearts lay; the countryside and to give them a better life away from the rigours of industrialised coastal town living.

George and Rose had reached their goals and for George now as a 'country copper', felt that he was in the 'right place' a selfless man standing head and shoulders within the community he proudly took under his wing, protecting it with enthusiasm and zeal. Now he could enjoy a good level of respect from the locals and as a big-hearted man with a firm approach would always help those in genuine need as did his loyal wife Rose.

PC George William Gutteridge had achieved so much in his, one could say sometimes 'colourful' and tragically short life but he remained true to himself, unpretentious, genuine, and selflessly loyal to his family and to the community on which he left a permanent, lasting and irreplaceable impression.

Bernard Mullin 2018

ACKNOWLEDGEMENTS

Mr Brian Alexander and family, first grandson of the late PC
George Gutteridge

Mr. Mark Alexander, great grandson of the late PC George
Gutteridge

Mrs Valerie Alexander.

The late Muriel and John Alexander

The Anglia Sign Casting Company, Horsford, Norwich

Mr Stephen Bailey, Chief Constable, Norfolk Constabulary

The Rev. Mike Banyard, Fordham Church, Cambs.

Matthew Clemenson and the Romford Recorder Newspaper
(Archant Ltd.)

Mrs Elizabeth Coon, Towneley Cottages, Tysea Hill St. Abbotts

Chief Superintendent, M. Sean 'O Callaghan, Divisional
Commander, Essex Constabulary

With grateful thanks to Dr Jo Chipperfield of New South Wales,
Australia for access to her complete doctoral thesis during my
research on The life of PC Gutteridge

Mrs Bernadette Dudney, Rise Park, Romford

The late Mr 'Titch' Dolman of St. Abbotts

The Essex Police Museum, Chelmsford and all of the staff for their
enthusiastic and very knowledgeable help in providing me on
many occasions with their time and access to the archived files
relating to the murder of PC Gutteridge most notably Martin
Stallion, Editor of The Police History Society Magazine

The Essex Records Office

The Essex Times

Essex Life Magazine

Mrs Marion Francis, for providing access to the Stapleford Abbotts History Society Archives

Mr Stephen Gutteridge and family, grandson of the late PC George Gutteridge

Mr Christopher Gutteridge and family, grandson of the late PC George Gutteridge

Mr Roy Gutteridge

PC Joseph Gutteridge, Norfolk Police

Mr Peter Gibson, T. Cribb and Son, Stapleford Abbotts

The Rev. Canon Roger Gayler, The Parochial Church Council and all members of the Church community of St. Mary the Virgin, St. Abbotts

Mr Ian Hatchman, Social Historian, North Weald, Essex

Jean Hancill of Durham Police

Hanna and colleagues at Braintree Cemetery

Mr Stephen Kavanagh, Chief Constable, Essex Constabulary

PC Jane Kimble, Essex Police, Epping

Inspector Martyn Lockwood, Researcher and Author, The Essex Police Museum

Norfolk Constabulary

Mrs Kay Pearce, St. Abbotts for access to the original Titch Dolman Tapes and helping to make this book possible

Mr Mrs B. Rogers of Stapleford Abbotts

Freda Rhodes, Daughter of 'Titch' Dolman

Mr Ray Russell, appointed church liason (bronze memorial)

Inspector Dr Maureen Scollan, Essex Police

Mrs Margaret Sutton, Towneley Cottages, Tysea Hill, St. Abbotts

Miss Tracey Sutton, Towneley Cottages, Tysea Hill, St. Abbotts

Mr Martin Stallion, Editor and Researcher, The Police History Society

The Triumph Owners Club of Great Britain

Mrs Becky Wash, Former Curator, The Essex Police Museum

Hanna Wilson, current Curator of the Essex Police Museum

Liz Whymark, St. Abbotts Village Hall

Mr Leonard Woodley, Membership Secretary, The Police History Society

Mrs Pamela Ward, daughter-in-law of Alec Ward

Mr John Ward, (recently and sadly deceased), last surviving son of Alec Ward

Quotes and source information, with grateful thanks.

BIBLIOGRAPHY

Ancestry.Com

Berry-Dee C., Odell R., 1993 The Long Drop. London: Virgin

Bunker J., 1988 From Rattle to Radio. Studley: Brewin

Brock A., 1948 A Casebook of Crime. London: Rockliff

The British Newspaper Archive

Chipperfield J., 2011 Naratives of crime and detection in interwar England: a case study of the murder of PC George Gutteridge. Sydney Australia

Mc. Connell J., 1976 The Detectives. London: David and Charles

Dilnot G., Triumphs of Detection. London: Bles

The archived material and quotes relating to the murder of PC Gutteridge, by kind courtesy of the Essex Police Museum, Chelmsford.

The Essex Times, Saturday 1st. October 1927

Emsley C., 2009 The Great British Bobby. London: Quercus

Furneaux R., 1962 They Died by a Gun. London: Mayflower-Dell

The Forest Town Heritage Group

Green N., Tough Times and Grisly Crimes: Nigel Green Media

Gribble L., 1971 Famous Detective Feats. London: Barker

Honeycomb G., 2009 Murders of the Black Museum. London: John Blake

Humphreys Sir T., 1953 a book of Trials. London: Heinemann

Humphreys C., 1931 Seven Murderers. London: Heinemann

Haweyes 1. Do You Have a Ghost Story ?

Kent Sylvia www.essexlifemagazine January 2008

Lane B., 1993 Chronicle of 20th Century Murder. London: Virgin

Lockwood M., 2009 The Essex Police force, A History. Stroud: The History Press

Laurence J., Extra Ordinary Crimes. London: Samson Low

Multiple authors, Famous Crimes of Recent Times. London: Newnes

Marples P., 2013 Clipstone Camp and the Mansfield Area in World War One:

Midsummer Books 1995 Real Life Crimes. London: Eaglemoss

Stevenson J., 1984 British Society 1914-45. London: Penguin

Scollan Dr M., Sworn to Serve, Police in Essex. Chichester Sussex: Phillimore.

Totterdell GHR., 1956 Country Copper. London: Harrap

Teignmouth Shore W., 1931 Crime and Its Detection. London: Gresham

Rowland D., 2008 Titch's Tale. St. Albans : Blenheim

Teignmouth Shore W., 1930 Trial of Browne and Kennedy. Edinburgh and London: Hodge

Pugh M., 2009 We Danced all Night. London: Vintage

Rowland D., 2008 Titch's Tale. St. Albans: Blenheim

Stratman L., 2011 More Essex Murders. Stroud: The History Press

Woodgate J., 1985 The Essex Police. Suffolk: Dalton

https://enwikipedia.org/windex.php?

Wikipedia.com.